Boston, 135 Washington Street,
March, 1851.

NEW BOOKS AND NEW EDITIONS

PUBLISHED BY

TICKNOR, REED, AND FIELDS.

HENRY W. LONGFELLOW'S WRITINGS.

Complete Poetical Works. This edition contains the six Volumes mentioned below, and is the only complete collection in the market. In two volumes, 16mo, $2.00.

In separate Volumes, each 75 cents.

VOICES OF THE NIGHT.
BALLADS and OTHER POEMS.
SPANISH STUDENT; A Play in Three Acts.
BELFRY OF BRUGES and OTHER POEMS.
EVANGELINE; a Tale of Acadie.
THE SEASIDE AND THE FIRESIDE.
THE WAIF. A Collection of Poems. Edited by Longfellow.
THE ESTRAY. A Collection of Poems. Edited by Longfellow.

MR. LONGFELLOW'S PROSE WORKS.

Hyperion. A Romance. In one volume, 16mo, price $1.00.

Outre-Mer. A Pilgrimage Beyond the Sea. In one volume, 16mo, price $1.00.

Kavanagh. A Tale. Lately published. In one vol. 16mo, price 75 cents.

NATHANIEL HAWTHORNE'S WRITINGS.

Twice-Told Tales. A New Edition. In two vols. 16mo, with Portrait, price $1.50.

The Scarlet Letter. A Romance. In one vol. 16mo, price 75 cents.

The House of the Seven Gables. In one volume, 16mo, price $1.00.

True Stories from History and Biography. In one volume, 16mo, with fine Engravings, price 75 cents.

JOHN G. WHITTIER'S WRITINGS.

OLD PORTRAITS AND MODERN SKETCHES. In one vol. 16mo. Just published, price 75 cents.

MARGARET SMITH'S JOURNAL. In one volume, 16mo, price 75 cents cloth, 50 cents in paper.

SONGS OF LABOR AND OTHER POEMS. In one volume, 16mo, price 50 cents.

OLIVER WENDELL HOLMES'S WRITINGS.

POEMS. In one volume, 16mo. New Edition, enlarged, with fine Portrait. Price $1.00.

ASTRÆA, THE BALANCE OF ILLUSIONS. In one vol. 16mo, price 25 cents.

ALFRED TENNYSON'S WRITINGS.

POEMS. A New Edition, enlarged, with Portrait. In two volumes, 16mo, price $1.50.

THE PRINCESS. A Medley. In one volume, 16mo, price 50 cents.

IN MEMORIAM. In one volume, 16mo, price 75 cents.

THOMAS DE QUINCEY'S WRITINGS.

CONFESSIONS OF AN ENGLISH OPIUM-EATER AND SUSPIRIA DE PROFUNDIS. In one volume, 16mo, price 75 cents.

BIOGRAPHICAL ESSAYS. In one volume, 16mo, price 75 cents.

MISCELLANEOUS ESSAYS. In one volume, 16mo, price 75 cents.

THE CÆSARS. In one volume, 16mo, price 75 cents.

GRACE GREENWOOD'S WRITINGS.

GREENWOOD LEAVES. A Collection of Stories and Letters. In one volume, 12mo. New Edition, price $1 25.

POEMS. In one volume, 16mo, with fine Portrait. Price 75 cents.

HISTORY OF MY PETS. A Book for Children. With fine Engravings. Price 50 cents.

EDWIN P. WHIPPLE'S WRITINGS.

Essays and Reviews. A New and Revised edition. In two volumes, 16mo, price $2.00.

Lectures on Subjects connected with Literature and Life. In one volume, 16mo, price 63 cents.

Washington and the Revolution. In one volume, 16mo, price 20 cents.

HENRY GILES'S WRITINGS.

Lectures, Essays, and Miscellaneous Writing Two volumes, 16mo, price $1.50.

Christian Thought on Life. In Twelve Discourses. In one volume, 16mo, price 75 cents.

WILLIAM MOTHERWELL'S WRITINGS.

Poems, Narrative and Lyrical. A New Edition, Enlarged. In one volume, 16mo, price 75 cents.

Minstrelsy, Ancient and Modern. In two vols. 16mo, price $1.50.

JAMES RUSSELL LOWELL'S WRITINGS.

Complete Poetical Works. Revised, with Additions. In two volumes, 16mo, price $1.50.

The Nooning. In one volume, 16mo. (Just ready.)

The Biglow Papers. In one vol. 16mo, 50 cents.

MISCELLANEOUS.

CHARLES SPRAGUE. Poetical and Prose Writings. With fine Portrait. In one volume, 16mo, price 75 cents.

JOHN G. SAXE. Humorous and Satirical Poems. In one volume, 16mo, price 50 cents.

ROBERT BROWNING. Complete Poetical Works. In two volumes, 16mo, price $2.00.

BARRY CORNWALL. English Songs and other Small Poems. Enlarged Edition. In one volume, 16mo.

RICHARD MONCKTON MILNES. Poems of Many Years. In one volume, 16mo, price 75 cents.

GOETHE'S WILHELM MEISTER. Translated by CARLYLE. In two volumes, 16mo.

GOETHE'S FAUST. Translated by HAYWARD. In one volume, 16mo. New Edition, price 75 cents.

CHARLES SUMNER. ORATIONS AND SPEECHES. In two volumes, 16mo, price $2.50.

GEORGE S. HILLARD. THE DANGERS AND DUTIES OF THE MERCANTILE PROFESSION. In one volume, 16mo, price 25 cents.

HORACE MANN. A FEW THOUGHTS FOR A YOUNG MAN. In one volume, 16mo, price 25 cents.

HENRY T. TUCKERMAN. POEMS. In one volume, 16mo.

PHILLIP JAMES BAILEY. THE ANGEL WORLD AND OTHER POEMS. In one volume, 16mo, price 50 cents.

F. W. P. GREENWOOD. SERMONS OF CONSOLATION. In one volume, 16mo, price $1.00.

MEMORY AND HOPE. A BOOK OF POEMS, REFERRING TO CHILDHOOD. In one volume, 8vo, price $2.00.

REJECTED ADDRESSES. By HORACE and JAMES SMITH. In one volume, 16mo, price 50 cents.

ALDERBROOK. By FANNY FORESTER. In two vols. 12mo, price $1.75.

THE BOSTON BOOK. BEING SPECIMENS OF METROPOLITAN LITERATURE. In one volume, 12mo, price $1 25.

HEROINES OF THE MISSIONARY ENTERPRISE. In one volume, 16mo, price 75 cents.

CHARACTERISTICS OF WOMEN. By Mrs. JAMESON. In one volume, 12mo, price $1.00.

ANGEL-VOICES; or WORDS OF COUNSEL FOR OVERCOMING THE WORLD. In one volume, 18mo, price 38 cents.

THE CONSTITUTION OF MAN. By GEORGE COMBE. 27th Edition. In one volume, 12mo, price 75 cents.

WARRENIANA. In one volume, 16mo.

MEMOIR OF THE BUCKMINSTERS, FATHER AND SON. By Mrs. LEE. In one volume, 12mo.

EACH OF THE ABOVE POEMS AND PROSE WRITINGS, MAY BE HAD IN VARIOUS STYLES OF HANDSOME BINDING.

With the regards of the author

Mary E Golden

from Mr Ellis

POEMS.

POEMS

BY

HENRY THEODORE TUCKERMAN.

BOSTON:
TICKNOR, REED, AND FIELDS.
MDCCCLI

Thurston, Torry & Emerson, Printers

CONTENTS.

SONNETS.

POEMS.

THE SPIRIT OF POETRY.

Source of the grand, the beautiful, the true,
Awake thy spell, thy sacred glow renew!
Teach me to trace the influence divine
That warms the hero and bedecks the shrine,
Steals, like a shadow, at the twilight hour,
Broods o'er the mountain, nestles in the flower,
Bold as the eagle, gentle as the dove,
To scale the stars or plume the wings of love!
Why go we forth, impatient to explore
The storied wonders of a distant shore,
Hallowed by peerless art and glory's tomb,
Or clad by warmer suns in richer bloom?
When on the ear first breaks the seaman's strain,
Blent with the clanking of the rising chain,

The dreary signal sounding to depart,
Each long wild cry thrills through the burdened heart,
Home visions, thrice endeared, usurp the place
Of foreign pictures, fancy loved to trace ;
Hope's siren voice becomes a mournful knell
When quivering lips breathe forth a long farewell;
But when sad thoughts are quelled, tears dashed away,
Old ocean greets us with his glistening spray,
And while around the sullen waters roll,
Their solemn murmur pacifies the soul.
O, it is glorious to sojourn awhile
Upon the trackless deep, to know its smile
At summer eve, when gorgeous sunsets throw
O'er the foam-crests an amethystine glow,
Through flying cloud-rifts watch the orbs on high,
Like angels' censers waving in the sky,
And hear the wind-hymns pealing loud and clear,
To sound their triumph o'er the boundless sphere ;
Or watch the moon hang soothingly above,
Like a pure crescent for the brow of love,
While her rays tremble on the ocean's breast,
Like childhood's locks by sportive airs caressed.
  And Earth's fair scenes — the river's lucent vase,
That mirrors mountains in its crystal face,
The autumn-tinted woods, whose branches sway
Like mighty hosts in festival array,

The cascade's anthem and the incense sweet
Wafted from thickets nestled at its feet,
The cloistral silence of the forest aisles,
And charms that live where floral beauty smiles,
Palms whose high tops the upper breezes woo,
And amber clouds that fleck a heaven of blue,
Are all symbolic to poetic sight
Of higher glory and supreme delight.
Who has looked forth upon a southern vale,
When o'er it sweeps Spring's renovating gale,
To wave the vine-stalks pendent from the trees,
Like garlands dallying with the sun and breeze,
Shake off the dewdrops in their jewelled pride,
From jasmin bud and aloe's thorny side,
Stir the meek violet in its dim retreat,
And die in zephyrs at the mountain's feet; —
Who that has rocked upon Lake George's tide,
When its clear ripples in the moonlight glide,
And heard, amid the hills and islets fair,
The bugle's echo wake the summer air;
Or stood on Ætna's brow at break of day,
When crimson lines first tinge the pearly gray,
While wreaths of smoke and lurid flames rose nigh,
Flashing like altar fires against the sky,
And streaming, with a wild and fitful glow,
O'er the black lava crags and glittering snow;

And who Niagara's loveliness has known,
The rainbow diadem, the emerald throne,
Nor felt thy spell each baser thought control,
And, with delicious awe, subdue the soul?
  And whence the pleasure sad and undefined,
That steals, like autumn twilight, through the mind,
From monuments of eld — the relics gray
Of men and eras long since passed away?
Visions of by-gone worlds in shadows throng
Through memory's vestibule, when night's calm song
Mingles its cadence with the moaning breeze
That stirs the weeds upon the crumbling frieze,
Plays o'er the prostrate column's fluted side
As painted lizards round it fearless glide,
Waves the untrodden grass that rankly grows
Over a buried city's long repose,
While every echo of our footsteps there
Fills the deep silence of the pulseless air.
'Tis the enchantment of poetic thought,
With such a magic charm divinely fraught,
As can resummon ages, spread once more
The ruined temple's gaily pictured floor,
Its arches rear, and bid the concave ring
With minstrel strains or priestly worshipping.
And thus Time's calm and mystic spirit calls
At midnight through the Coliseum's walls,

Or in the old cathedral's mellow air
The musing stranger lures to silent prayer,
Weaves moss upon the rocks, with ivy twines
War's mouldering tower and Faith's deserted shrines,
Smooths the carved line, imprints the forehead meek,
Silvers the hair and pales the glowing cheek.
And would ye feel the sacred charm of Art,
Prove its poetic empire o'er the heart?
Beneath the unpillared dome go stand and gaze,
As o'er its frescos sunshine faintly plays;
See genius radiant with immortal grace,
Beaming so godlike from Apollo's face,
And Mary's smile, by Raphael's touch beguiled,
Bent in meek gladness on her slumbering child,
The poor, forgiven one, with golden hair
Gemmed by the dewdrops of subdued despair; [1]
Or Egypt's queen in orient beauty drest,
Holding the viper to her snowy breast.
Nor gaze alone, let thine enchanted ear
Catch every note that music scatters near;
When the soft echo of the village bell,
Or peasant's reed comes floating down the dell,
When winter gales, with leafless boughs at play,
Wake dirges wild to mourn the year's decay,
And sylvan choristers, in myriad tones,
Welcome back summer to the northern zones;

Or when some queen of sweet Euterpe's train,
Pours forth her spirit to a master strain,
How quickly high, impassioned fancies rise,
Arrayed in melody's ethereal guise!
Won from our clay, without death's fearful strife,
We taste the glories of poetic life.
Divine Bellini! as I wandered o'er
The fertile valleys of thy native shore,
Each crystal wave upheaving seemed to sigh
For the lost harp whose strains can never die:
Though cold thy brow beneath the laurel crown,
Thy country's name enshrines thy young renown,
Thy melody, in tones of fervent truth,
Embalms the ardor of thy gifted youth;
There the soul triumphs, vanished bliss deplores,
With joy exults, in adoration soars,
Freedom's appeal sweeps every heart along,
And love's own rapture gushes forth in song.
O for a lyre of melody profound,
That I might sing the poetry of sound!
That thrilling language worthy to unroll
The deep emotions of an earnest soul,
On which glad angels from the realms above,
Brought to the earth their embassy of love,
Whose airy spell in Miriam's triumph rose,
And won from Saul the memory of his woes;

Cheered Milton's blindness, harmonized his lays,
And wove a charm for Mary's captive days;[2]
Love's true expression caught from young Mozart,
And drove death's shadow from his trembling heart.[3]
O, if there be an art familiar here,
Whose welcome waits us in a higher sphere,
'Tis that which now so winningly reveals
All that the fancy paints or spirit feels.
Hence we invoke the moving grace of song,
When stars or clouds around our pathway throng;
Kindle young valor by the trumpet's note,
And from the lute bid love's soft pleadings float,
Wake holy musing in the organ's peal,
And joy's blithe echo from the clarion steal,
Cheer the bride's visions, ere in sleep they fade,
With the sweet cadence of the serenade,
And to the altar move with measured tread,
To breathe a requiem o'er the honored dead.
  There are who all poetic worship deem
The vague conception of an idle dream,
All hues romantic dash away with scorn,
As sickly mists of morbid fancy born;
Would quench in years the spirit's richest gift,
And wed brave manhood to ignoble thrift,
Boast of the age when reason's cool defence
Can vanquish sentiment by common sense,

And feeling's pristine earnestness control
By the firm barrier of a frozen soul,
Draw down blithe fancy from her joyous flight,
And still the music of unsought delight:
Not such the faith which court and tented glade
Cherished through ages lost in mental shade,
Nor such the hope of that immortal day
That ancient bards have rescued from decay,
When for poetic empire sages strove,
In temple porch and academic grove,
The free and patient votaries of Truth
Invoking reverence for the dreams of youth.
Each has his pharos; — some the twinkling ray
Of glow-worm joys that glimmer by the way,
Thought's prime apostates who profess to be
Vibrating ever from repose to glee,
All buoyant float down life's tumultuous stream,
And hail each bubble's transitory gleam;
Others, of deeper mood, compelled to think,
Their vassal natures to a dogma link,
By meteors led, and, like the quarry slave,
Dig in Opinion's mine a living grave,
Or tamely drudge where'er the mass may lead,
And swear allegiance to the reigning creed;
While the false flame and serpent-woven fold
Of Appetite, a baser order mould.

Though lofty hopes and fancies high and free
Oft wage relentless war with destiny,
Heed not the voice that bids thee turn aside
And yield life's crowning grace to worldly pride;
With calm devotion to this solace cling,
And trust thy soul to its angelic wing,
And as the sun upon an ice-clad scene,
Pours golden radiance, dazzling yet serene,
Earth's cold arena and life's melting ties,
Warm with effulgence borrowed from the skies!
  Alas! that as the strains of childhood's lute
Pass into hoarser music, or grow mute,
The light that made existence half divine,
Should fade unheeded from the spirit's shrine!
And yet, in after years, when falls the tear
O'er joy's dregged chalice or ambition's bier,
We seek the fount whose bright and fragrant shower
Cooled our flushed brows in being's morning hour,
And whose sweet murmur filled the heart of youth,
With the deep tones of Nature's living truth.
We live to see our fondest dreams betrayed,
And sadly watch each hopeful vision fade,
Yet, still assured, bid fresh illusions spring,
And to the promise of the future cling;
Nay, on the shadows of departed days,
Delight to cast Imagination's rays,

And seasons all unheeded in their flow,
Learn to contemplate with affection's glow.
Thus the blest spirit that I sing can lend
New charms to hope, with memory's visions blend,
Call back the smiles of days forever fled,
Round time to come benign allurements shed,
Grief's misty shades and pleasure's burning sun,
By a celestial arch, unite in one,
And to the gladdened pilgrim's weary eye,
Reveal the rainbow of life's troubled sky.
  How soon would custom disenchant the earth,
Bid wonder cease, and quench the zest of mirth,
Did thy sweet voice not mingle with our strife,
And oft revive the miracle of life!
As the dim pavement rich in ancient hues,
When sprinkled o'er, its primal tint renews,
So freshens Nature as thy holy tears
Baptize the soul and melt the frost of years.
Benignant spirit! still thy smile impart,
Exalt the mind and renovate the heart,
Some better moments let us cherish still,
Some flowers spare our shattered urns to fill,
Hallow and cheer a few green spots below,
Where love can meditate and fancy glow,
Where at thy shrine a vigil we may keep,
And feel our lives are "rounded with a sleep!"[4]

There lies a land far down a southern sea,
Whose air, though balmy, is no longer free ;
The briny gale and mountain's cordial breath
Circle a race that sleep in civic death,
Yet matchless graces to that sleep belong,
For o'er it floats the atmosphere of song.
Though withered crones sit spinning in the sun,
Where Cæsar's rule and Tully's fame begun,
Though moaning beggars crowd the fair domain,
And bigot priests usurp a pampered reign,
Still Beauty lives, enamored of the clime,
And twines her garlands round the wrecks of time ;
Drives from the patriot's brow its hopeless gloom,
With light that streams from Dante's lonely tomb,
Bids him, the airy dome beholding nigh,
Hail Angelo a tenant of the sky,
Muse on the trophies by the Dorian shore,
Columbus bravely won and sadly wore,
Or Galileo's honored name revere,
Borne on the rays of every golden sphere.
Poetic charms the peasant's olive face,
In Arno's vale, adorn with placid grace,
Flash from Venetian oars that tuneful sway,
When moonlight gilds the Adriatic bay,
With warlike memories stir the verdant grain
That waves luxuriant on the Lombard plain,

Waft citron blossoms, as the vesper bell
Dies faintly down Palermo's golden shell,
O'er sweet Parthenope in triumph stream,
Like beacon flames, in each volcanic gleam,
Brood in the stillness of Rome's saintly piles,
And scent the breeze from Como's fairy isles.
Read the great law in Beauty's cheering reign,
Blent with all ends through matter's wide domain;
She breathes hope's language, and with boundless range
Sublimes all forms, smiles through each subtle change,
And with insensate elements combined,
Ordains their constant ministry to mind.
The breeze awoke to waft the feathered seed,
And the cloud fountains with their dew to feed,
Upon it many errands might have flown,
Nor woke one river song or forest moan,
Stirred not the grass, nor the tall grain have bent,
Like shoreless billows tremulously spent;
Frost could the bosom of the lake have glassed,
Nor paused to paint the woodland as it passed,
The glossy seabird and the brooding dove
Might coyly peck, with twinkling eye of love,
Nor catch upon their downy necks the dyes
So like the mottled hues of summer skies;
Mists in the west could float, nor glory wear,
As if an angel's robes were streaming there;

The moon might sway the tides, nor yet impart
A solemn light to tranquillize the heart,
And leagues of sand could bar the ocean's swell,
Nor yield one crystal gleam or pearly shell.
The very sedge lends music to the blast,
And the thorn glistens when the storm is past,
Wild flowers nestle in the rocky cleft,
Moss decks the bough of leaf and life bereft,
O'er darkest clouds the moonbeams brightly steal,
The rainbow's herald is the thunder's peal;
Gay are the weeds that strew the barren shore,
And anthem-like the breaker's gloomy roar;
As love o'er sorrow spreads her genial wings,
The ivy round a fallen column clings,
While on the sinking walls, where owlets cry,
The weather-stains in tints of beauty lie;
The wasting elements adorn their prey,
And throw a pensive charm around decay;
Thus ancient limners bade their canvass glow,
And grouped sweet cherubs o'er a martyr's wo.
  Nor does the charm of poetry disdain
In forms instinctive to assert her reign;
With graceful sweep the startled curlews fly,
And the struck deer will turn aside to die;
How moves the steed majestical and free,
How builds the beaver, and how stores the bee!

The patient glow-worm lights a torch of love,
And to her goal flies on the faithful dove,
Rare colors o'er the dying dolphin play,
And coral groves an insect's art betray.
But not alone where verdure, wave and sky
Serenely blend to captivate the eye,
In the still woods or soothing voice of streams
Does poetry derive her moving themes.
The city mark, its motley crowd survey,
Decked with the trophies of blind Fortune's sway;
Trace the procession mingling from afar,
The gaudy chariot and the funeral car,
The tattered wretch, the belle in proud array,
The anxious plodder and the child at play.
Walk by the port, at sunset, to descry
A leafless forest painted on the sky,
Those masts are winged triumphantly to sweep
The cold gray bosom of the mighty deep,
Spread wisdom's beams, dissevered worlds unite,
Trade's guerdon win, or dare the billowy fight,
Each nation's ensign rear to foreign gales,
And whiten ocean with a thousand sails.
At eve, the lights from every casement shed
Illume the feast or glimmer o'er the dead,
Shine on a band who mutual blessings share,
Or mock the haggard visage of despair;

Here the pleased infant's wondering sight engage,
And there proclaim the vigil of the sage:
The gable roof and lofty palace door,
The ancient spire with moonbeams silvered o'er,
The sunken tombstone and the cheerful street
Humanity's great lesson still repeat.
And home's calm privacy thy presence cheers,
To wake its smiles and consecrate its tears.
We trace thee in the harp, the vase, the bust
That calls the dear departed from the dust,
The pictured ceiling and mosaic floor,
The woodbine trained around the cottage door,
The sculptured chalice brimmed with sparkling wine,
And "flow of soul" that makes the feast divine.
And when the eye can scan thy gifts no more,
When fancy's revel on the earth is o'er,
In some blest spot where groups of noble trees
Spread their dense foliage to the summer breeze;
Where the oak yields its rich autumnal hue,
And drip the pine leaves with the morning dew,
Where moans the cypress, or the lindens wave,
Allured by thee we find a quiet grave.
At Père là Chaise thy holy genius dwells,
Hangs on each cross a wreath of *immortels*,
And thy bright dreams with hopeful emblems fill
The shades of Auburn and fair Laurel Hill;

Through the dark firs a pyramid behold,
On which the patriot's sacred deeds are told,
A broken shaft speaks of departed youth,
And a white urn proclaims a maiden's truth;
By the dark portal of the silent tomb,
The wild birds warble and the roses bloom,
Poetic graces round the scene are shed,
And beauty cheers a city of the dead.
  How vain the toil that dims the eye of youth,
To garner barren words in search of truth!
What can avail the gems of choicest lore,
If the pale student does but count them o'er,
Like miser's coin, and lacks the sacred flame
That wreathes with living light each hallowed name,
Displays on fancy's flowers truth's crystal dew,
Draws from each pearl of thought its richest hue,
Blends scattered beauties, and on wisdom's scroll
Pours the full radiance of a kindred soul?
Transmuting spirit! in thy magic fold
Thought's common dross is changed to virgin gold;
Chartered by thee, how deeply we engage
In the rich pathos of the tragic page;
With Hamlet muse, share Richard's dream of fear,
Bend with Cordelia o'er reviving Lear,
Imbibe Othello's fierce and fond despair,
Or breathe with Juliet love's ecstatic air!

And what is History unadorned by thee?
An arid path, a shadow-vested sea,
Tales of a bigot's wiles, a tyrant's frown,
Heartless espousals to secure a crown,
War after war, and reign succeeding reign,
A monarch's pleasure and a people's bane:
Thy holy radiance plays not o'er the spot,
Where kings were idolized and men forgot,
But fondly lingers round the Alpine dell,
In whose sweet echo lives the name of Tell,
And lights the forest gloom where, undismayed,
The Indian girl her father's vengeance stayed,
And bowed her head to take the savage blow
Destined to lay a captive stranger low;
Or, like a star, eternal vigil keeps
Where our world-honored, angel-hero sleeps.
Life's mighty sorrows, by profound appeal,
High consolation to the soul reveal;
In the fierce onset, his expiring breath,
All unawares, the warrior yields to death,
And Fortune's child, when from her temple hurled,
Will bear a dauntless presence through the world;
Roused by the rudeness of the sudden shock,
Scorns pity, laughs at fate, and, like a rock
Lashed by the surges on life's dreary shore,
Stands firm and lone till changeful time is o'er:

And they who see the dread sepulchral sleep
O'er all their loved ones unrelenting creep,
With firm endurance meet the fatal strokes,
Like storm-scathed hills or thunder-riven oaks;
But milder sufferings, more enduring wo,
That, like Tophana's waters, poison slow,[5]
Bring no excitement potent to sustain,
Inciting courage and absorbing pain.
Such is his lot in fragile frame arrayed,
On whom disease her solemn hand has laid;
Like a blithe bird with arrow-shivered plume,
Confined to lowly flights and narrow doom,
Fated to watch his mates with drooping eye,
Circle triumphant through the glowing sky,
Fast moored his bark with adamantine chain,
Impatient heaves to tempt the open main;
And if the notes of Fame's melodious horn
Make his heart leap in manhood's eager morn,
A fluttering pulse or throb of anguish wild,
Mocks the frail hope that to his fancy smiled:
Ah! not for him does pleasure twine her flowers.
In festive hall, or laughter-ringing bowers;
The charm of wit and love's Elysian strain
Dispelled by trembling nerve or aching brain;
And if the thrill bid rapture's fountains flow,
How shadow-like 'tis followed by the throe!

How dark a lot were being such as this,
If unattended by poetic bliss!
Yet thus consoled, lone suffering's patient child,
Of pain and weariness full oft beguiled,
Asks for no throne but his accustomed chair,
Nor rarer blessings than he summons there;
With half closed eyes, in musing pleasure lost,
Dissolves in dreams Time's devastating frost,
Or roaming forth to court the zephyr's play,
Noon's balmy softness floating round his way,
The rare communion quickens every vein
With rapturous sense of Nature's blissful reign.
Pause at this threshold; shade thy weary eye,
Sated with light from Rome's cerulean sky.[6]
Yon flame that half illumes the dusky room,
A low watch-tick, and flowers' faint perfume
Alone give sign of life; approach and bend
O'er the low couch, to mark a poet's end:
No wife stands by, with deep but chastened wo,
To soothe death's stern and desolating throe,
No sister's face or father's form revered,
By a long ministry of love endeared,
Are there, his final agony to cheer
With kindly word or sympathizing tear,
Bathe his parched lips, his cold hand fondly press,
And Heaven invoke the parting soul to bless:

From a mere boy he loved the Grecian streams,
Sappho's high strain and Plato's mystic dreams,
Fables that live on Homer's deathless page,
And all the wonders of the classic age:
He pondered on its beauty till there grew
A passion those rare graces to renew,
And for such strains his harp he boldly strung,
E'en to the accents of a northern tongue;
The aim was lofty, worthy life's proud dawn,
Nobler than common themes of fashion born;
The Muses smiled when Genius gave it birth,
But critics coldly laughed with scornful mirth;
The poet's eye grew bright with hectic fire,
And Hope's cold visage stilled his trembling lyre;
He sought the breezes of a southern sky,
From home and country roamed, alone to die;
Yet one consoler cheered his latest breath,
And smoothed the pathway of an exile's death;
The tuneful bird in boyhood's breast that sang
Still charmed to silence every earthly pang;
E'en in that vale of shadows lone and drear,
Herald of coming joy, yet warbled near;
The setting sun, before his waning gaze,
Upon the curtain poured his crimson rays,
And as they glowed, then quivered, faded, fled,
Calmly the dying poet turned his head;

" And such is life," he whispered in the ear
Of the one friend, who watchful lingered near,
" With me 'tis done ; write on my early tomb
My name was writ in water, flowers bloom
Over my ashes — death's dew is on my brow —
My heart grows still — and yet I feel them now ! "
Heroic guide ! whose wings are never furled,
By thee Spain's voyager sought another world ;
What but poetic impulse could sustain
That dauntless pilgrim on the dreary main ?
Day after day his mariners protest,
And gaze with dread along the pathless west ;
Beyond that realm of waves untracked before,
Thy fairy pencil traced the promised shore,
Through weary storms and faction's fiercer rage,
The scoffs of ingrates and the chills of age,
Thy voice renewed his earnestness of aim,
And whispered pledges of eternal fame,
Thy cheering smile atoned for fortune's frown,
And made his fetters garlands of renown.
Princes, when softened in thy sweet embrace,
Yearn for no conquest but the realm of grace,
And thus redeemed, Lorenzo's fair domain
Smiled in the light of Art's propitious reign.
Delightful Florence ! though the northern gale
Will sometimes rave around thy lovely vale,

Can I forget how softly Autumn threw
Beneath thy skies, her robes of ruddy hue,
Through what long days of balminess and peace,
From wintry bonds Spring won thy mild release?
Along the Arno then I loved to pass,
And watch the violets peeping from the grass,
Mark the gray kine each chestnut grove between,
Startle the pheasants on the lawny green,
Or down long vistas hail the mountain snow,
Like lofty shrines the purple cloud below.
Within thy halls, when veiled the sunny rays,
Marvels of art await the ardent gaze,
And liquid words from lips of beauty start,
With social joy to warm the stranger's heart.
How beautiful, at moonlight's hallowed hour,
Thy graceful bridges, and celestial tower!
The girdling hills enchanted seem to hang
Round the fair scene whence modern genius sprang;
O'er the dark ranges of thy palace walls
The silver beam on dome and cornice falls;
The statues clustered in thy ancient square
Like mighty spirits print the solemn air,
Silence meets beauty with unbroken reign,
Save when invaded by a choral strain,
Whose distant cadence falls upon the ear,
To fill the bosom with poetic cheer.

For Fame life's meaner records vainly strive,
While, in fresh beauty, thy high dreams survive:
Still Vesta's temple throws its classic shade
O'er the bright foam of Tivoli's cascade,
And to one Venus still we bow the knee,
Divine as if just issued from the sea;
In fancy's trance, yet deem on nights serene,
We hear the revels of the fairy queen,
That Dian's smile illumes the marble fane,
And Ceres whispers in the rustling grain,
That Ariel's music has not died away,
And in his shell still floats the Culprit Fay.[7]
The sacred beings of poetic birth
Immortal live to consecrate the earth.
San Marco's pavement boasts no Doge's tread,
And all its ancient pageantry has fled;
Yet as we muse beneath some dim arcade,
The mind's true kindred glide from ruin's shade:
In every passing eye that sternly beams,
We start to meet the Shylock of our dreams;
Each maiden form, where virgin grace is seen,
Crosses our path with Portia's noble mien,
While Desdemona, beauteous as of yore,
Yields us the smile that once entranced the Moor.
How Scotland's vales are peopled to the heart
By her bold minstrel's necromantic art!

Along this fern moved Jeannie's patient feet,
Where hangs yon mist, rose Ellangowan's seat,
Here the sad bride first gave her love a tongue,
And there the chief's last shout of triumph rung ;
Beside each stream, down every glen they throng,
The cherished offspring of creative song !
Long ere brave Nelson shook the Baltic shore,
The bard of Avon hallowed Elsinore :
Perchance when moored the fleet, awaiting day,
To fix the battle's terrible array,
Some pensive hero, musing o'er the deep,
So soon to fold him in its dreamless sleep,
Heard the Dane's sad and self-communing tone
Blend with the water's melancholy moan,
Recalled, with prayer and awe-suspended breath,
His wild and solemn questionings of death,
Or caught from land Ophelia's dying song
Swept by the night-breeze plaintively along !
What charms on motion can thy grace bestow,
To sway the willow or to wreath the snow,
Bow the ripe maize like golden spears that fall,
With one accord to greet their leader's call,
Twirl the red leaf in circles through the air,
Or guide the torrent to its foaming lair :
E'en the rude billows, wafted by thy hand,
With sweep majestic break along the strand,

And downy clouds that cluster in the west,
Seem winged with hope like spirits of the blest.
Thine is the spell that quickens buoyant feet,
In the gay onset and the coy retreat,
Through fairy mazes that bewitch the sight,
And sprightly rounds prolific of delight,
Till the blithe magic every sense entrance,
And lead us captives to the joyous dance.
  And Love, that, like the lily, meekly rears
Her vernal joy above the flood of years,
Flits round our path till shadowed by the grave,
As ocean-birds skim o'er the gloomy wave,
How rich her gifts, how seraph-like her guise,
When on poetic wing she nobly flies!
Then, in the virgin brow, we joy to find
A lovely emblem of congenial mind,
Hail feeling in the dimpling lips that part
To free the beatings of the quickened heart,
While each kind word that from them softly falls,
Thrills every pulse as when a trumpet calls;
Or meet the eye, affection's beaming goal,
To feel the presence of congenial soul,
Caress each ringlet of the flowing hair,
As it were charmed to lure us from despair,
And round a human idol trembling throw
All the fond hopes on which we live below!

Nor time, nor care, nor death have power to tame
Our votive trust, or dim the quenchless flame.
Cheered by its light, the Tuscan muse defied
Exile and hardship, courtly pomp and pride,
Through the cold mists neglect around him threw,
And storms of hate that o'er him fiercely blew,
A presence saw, the brooding clouds above,
The changeless presage of eternal love!
And that pale face, bowed on the open leaf,
Whence its bland air of subjugated grief? [8]
Methinks 'tis strange that death should gently steal,
And, like a slumber, life's warm fountain seal,
Just as its last clear droppings shrunk away
To their clear well-spring, from the light of day;
Thus Laura's bard in peaceful musing died,
A life poetic closed, by love beatified.
  On Judah's hills thy effluence hovered nigh,
As Bethlehem's star wheeled up the tranquil sky,
And holy grew where on his sinless breast,
A Saviour bade the head of childhood rest.
Spirit of faith! to whose pure source we turn,
When hopes divine with holiest rapture burn,
Can reason follow thy seraphic feet
Beyond the world, to God's eternal seat?
Dear as thy promise is, O what wert thou,
Could we not image thy memorials now,

And in exalted mood delight to trace
The unseen glories of thy dwelling-place?
Consoling spirit! Eden's peerless bird!
Thy melody to loftiest musing stirred
The sightless minstrel, and thy sacred spell
Brought peace to Cowper, gladdened Tasso's cell,
Attuned the harp of Burns to strains which bear
No transient rapture to the sons of care,
Cheered the brave Korner through that weary night
Whose dreams presaged the issue of the fight,
Scott's votive steps allured to Melrose gray,
Whose pensive beauty woke his noble lay,
From sorrow's thrall gave Hemans sweet release,
And Byron armed to war for conquered Greece,
Forever green bade Goldsmith's hawthorn wave,[9]
And wreathed the surge o'er Shelley's ocean-grave!
And some upon our free Atlantic shore,
Redeeming spirit, thy domain explore,
In deathless marble lines of beauty trace,
Or weave in language images of grace;
Like Allston, silent poetry infuse
Through speaking forms, and more than living hues;
With Irving's diction noble thoughts prolong,
Or follow Bryant through the maze of song.
Celestial gift! whene'er entranced we feel
Thy sacred rapture o'er our spirits steal,

From morn's rich beauty, evening's sweet repose,
The gleam of dew, or bloom of vernal rose ;
Whether thy greeting come in music rare,
Or on the balm that scents the summer air,
Speak in the artist's touch, the minstrel's tone,
Or in the poet's thought — thy secret throne,
Lurk in the grove, or cloud's refulgent dress,
The ocean's roar, or zephyrs' soft caress ;
Whether thy smile illume the midnight sky,
Or, all concentered, beam from woman's eye,
Thou art the chosen herald from above,
And thy eternal message — God is Love.

NOTES.

Note 1. Page 5.

The poor forgiven one with golden hair,
Gemmed with the dewdrops of subdued despair.

The Magdalens of the old masters are almost invariably represented with light-colored tresses — "brown in the shadow, and gold in the sun."

Note 2. Page 7.

And wove a charm for Mary's captive days.

The captivity of the unfortunate Queen of Scots was often beguiled by her lute.

Note 3. Page 7.

Love's true expression caught from young Mozart,
And drove Death's shadow from his trembling heart.

One of Mozart's finest compositions was inspired by his love for Constance Weber. The circumstances under which his celebrated Requiem were written, are well known.

Note 4. Page 10.

And feel our lives are rounded with a sleep.

We are such stuff
As dreams are made of, and our little life
Is rounded with a sleep.

Tempest, Act iv., Sc. 1.

NOTE 5. Page 18.

But milder suffering, more enduring wo
That, like Tophana's waters, poison slow.

Tophana flourished in the latter part of the seventeenth century. She prepared a delicate compound of arsenic, which entered freely into commerce, and was known under the name of *acqua della Toffana.*

NOTE 6. Page 19.

Pause at this threshold; shade thy weary eye,
Sated with light from Rome's cerulean sky.

See MILNE'S LIFE OF KEATS.

NOTE 7. Page 23.

And in his shell still floats the Culprit Fay.

See Drake's Poem, "THE CULPRIT FAY."

NOTE 8. Page 26.

And that pale face bowed on the open leaf,
Whence its bland air of subjugated grief?

Petrarch was found dead in his library, apparently asleep — his head resting on an open book.

NOTE 9. Page 27.

Forever green, bade Goldsmith's hawthorn wave.

The hawthorn bush, with seats beneath the shade,
For talking age and whispering lovers made.

THE DESERTED VILLAGE.

THE APOLLO BELVIDERE.

There is a tradition at Rome, that an imaginative French girl died of love for this celebrated statue.

It was a day of festival in Rome,
And to the splendid temple of her saint,
Many a brilliant equipage swept on ;
Brave cavaliers reined their impetuous steeds,
While dark-robed priests and bright-eyed peasants strolled,
Through groups of citizens, in gay attire.
The suppliant moan of the blind mendicant,
Blent with the huckster's cry, the urchin's shout,
The clash of harness, and the festive cheer.
Beneath the colonnade ranged the Swiss guards,
With polished halberds — an anomaly,
Of mountain lineage, and yet hirelings!
In the midst rose the majestic obelisk,
Quarried in Egypt, centuries by-gone ;
And, on either side, gushed up refreshingly

The lofty fountains, flashing in the sun,
And breathing, o'er the din, a whisper soft,
Yet finely musical as childhood's laugh.
Here a stranger stood in mute observance;
There an artist leaned, and pleased his eye
With all the features of the shifting scene,
Striving to catch its varying light and shade —
The mingled tints of brilliancy and gloom.
Through the dense crowd a lovely maiden pressed
With a calm brow, an eagerness of air,
And an eye exultant with high purpose.
The idle courtier checked his ready jest,
And backward stepped in reverence, as she passed;
The friar turned and blessed her fervently,
Reading the joy in her deep look of love,
That visits pilgrims when their shrine is won.
To the rich chambers of the Vatican
She hurried thoughtfully, nor turned to muse
Upon the many glories clustered there.
There are rooms whose walls are radiant still
With the creations of the early dead —
Raphael, the gifted and the beautiful;
Fit places those for sweet imaginings
And spirit-stirring dreams. She entered not.
Gems of rare hues and cunning workmanship,
Ancient sarcophagi, heroic forms,

Busts of the mighty conquerors of time,
Stirred not a pulse in that fond maiden's heart;
She staid not to peruse the classic face
Of young Augustus, nor lingered to discern
Benignity in Trajan's countenance;
But sped, with fawn-like and familiar step,
On to the threshold of a cabinet;
And then her eye grew brighter, and a flush
Suffused her cheek, as, awe-subdued, she paused,
And, throwing back the ringlets from her brow,
With a light bound and rapturous murmur, stood
Before the statue of the Grecian god:

"They tell me thou art stone,
Stern, passionless, and chill,
Dead to the glow of noble thought,
And feeling's holy thrill;
They deem thee but a marble god,
The paragon of art,
A thing to charm the sage's eye,
But not to win the heart.

"Vain as their own light vows,
And soulless as their gaze,
The thought of quenching my deep love
By such ignoble praise!

I know that through thy parted lips
Language disdains to roll,
While on them rest so gloriously
The beamings of the soul.

"I dreamed, but yesternight,
That, gazing, e'en as now,
Rapt in a wild, admiring joy,
On thy majestic brow—
That thy strong arm was round me flung,
And drew me to thy side,
While thy proud lip uncurled in love,
And hailed me as a bride.

"And then, methought, we sped,
Like thine own arrow, high,
Through fields of azure, orbs of light,
Amid the boundless sky:
Our way seemed walled with radiant gems,
As fell the starry gleams,
And the floating isles of pearly drops
Gave back their silver beams.

"Sphere-music, too, stole by
In the fragrant zephyr's play,
And the hum of worlds boomed solemnly
Across our trackless way:

Upon my cheek the wanton breeze
Thy glowing tresses flung ;
Like loving tendrils, round my neck,
A golden band they clung.

" Methought thou didst impart
The mysteries of earth,
And whisper lovingly the tale
Of thy celestial birth :
O'er Poetry's sublimest heights
Exultingly we trod ;
Thy words were music — uttering
The genius of a god !

" Proud one ! 'twas but a dream ;
For here again thou art,
Thy marble bosom heeding not
My passion-stricken heart.
O, turn that rapturous look on me,
And heave a single sigh —
Give but a glance, breathe but a tone,
One word were ecstasy !

" Still mute ? Then must I yield :
This fire will scathe my breast ;
This weary heart will throb itself
To an eternal rest.

Yet still my soul claims fellowship
  With the exalted grace,
The bright and thrilling earnestness,
  The godlike in thy face.

"Thou wilt relent at last,
  And turn thy love-lit eye
In pity on me, noble one!
  To bless me ere I die.
And now, farewell, my vine-clad home,
  Farewell, immortal youth!
Let me behold thee when Love calls
  The martyr to her truth!"

MARY.

WHAT though the name is old and oft repeated,
  What though a thousand beings bear it now;
And true hearts oft the gentle word have greeted,—
  What though 'tis hallowed by a poet's vow?
We ever love the rose, and yet its blooming
  Is a familiar rapture to the eye,
And yon bright star we hail, although its looming
  Age after age has lit the northern sky.

As starry beams o'er troubled billows stealing,
  As garden odors to the desert blown,
In bosoms faint a gladsome hope revealing,
  Like patriot music or affection's tone—
Thus, thus for aye, the name of Mary spoken
  By lips or text, with magic-like control,
The course of present thought has quickly broken,
  And stirred the fountains of my inmost soul.

The sweetest tales of human weal and sorrow,
  The fairest trophies of the limner's fame,
To my fond fancy, Mary, seem to borrow
  Celestial halos from thy gentle name:
The Grecian artist gleaned from many faces,
  And in a perfect whole the parts combined,
So have I counted o'er dear woman's graces
  To form the Mary of my ardent mind.

And marvel not I thus call my ideal,
  We inly paint as we would have things be,
The fanciful springs ever from the real,
  As Aphrodite rose from out the sea;
Who smiled upon me kindly day by day,
  In a far land where I was sad and lone?
Whose presence now is my delight alway?
  Both angels must the same blessed title own.

What spirits round my weary way are flying,
  What fortunes on my future life await,
Like the mysterious hymns the winds are sighing,
  Are all unknown, — in trust I bide my fate;
But if one blessing I might crave from Heaven,
  'T would be that Mary should my being cheer,
Hang o'er me when the chord of life is riven,
  Be my dear household word, and my last accent here.

NORTHAMPTON.

Ere from thy calm seclusion parted,
  O fairest village of the plain!
The thoughts that here to life have started
  Draw me to Nature's heart again.

The tasseled maize, full grain or clover,
  Far o'er the level meadow grows,
And through it, like a wayward rover,
  The noble river gently flows.

Majestic elms, with trunks unshaken
  By all the storms an age can bring,
Trail sprays whose rest the zephyrs waken,
  Yet lithesome with the juice of spring.

By sportive airs the foliage lifted,
  Each green leaf shows its white below,
As foam on emerald waves is drifted,
  Their tints alternate come and go.

And then the skies! when vapors cluster
  From zenith to horizon's verge,
As wild gusts ominously bluster,
  And in deep shade the landscape merge;—

Under the massive cloud's low border,
  Where hill-tops with the sky unite,
Like an old minster's blazoned warder,
  There scintillates an amber light:

Sometimes a humid fleece reposes
  Midway upon the swelling ridge,
Like an aerial couch of roses,
  Or fairy's amethystine bridge:

And pale green inlets lucid shimmer,
  With huge cliffs jutting out beside,
Like those in mountain lakes that glimmer,
  Tinged like the ocean's crystal tide:

Or saffron-tinted islands planted
  In firmaments of azure dye,
With pearly mounds that loom undaunted,
  And float like icebergs of the sky:

Like autumn leaves that eddying falter,
  Yet settle to their crimson rest,
As pilgrims round their burning altar,
  They slowly gather in the west.

And when the distant mountain ranges
  In moonlight or blue mist or clad,
Oft memory all the landscape changes,
  And pensive thoughts are blent with glad.

For then, as in a dream Elysian,
  Val d'Arno's fair and loved domain
Seems, to my rapt yet waking vision,
  To yield familiar charms again.

Save that for dome and turret hoary,
  Amid the central valley lies
A white church-spire unknown to story,
  And smoke-wreaths from a cottage rise.

On Holyoke's summit woods are frowning,
  No line of cypresses we see,
Nor convent old with beauty crowning
  The heights of sweet Fiesole.

Yet here may willing eyes discover
  The art and life of every shore,
For Nature bids her patient lover
  All true similitudes explore.

These firs, when cease their boughs to quiver,
  Stand like pagodas brahmins seek,
Yon isle, that parts the winding river,
  Seems moulded from a light caique.

And ferns that in these groves are hidden,
  Are sculptured like a dainty frieze,
While choral music steals unbidden,
  As undulates the forest breeze.

A gothic arch and springing column,
  A floral-dyed, mosaic ground,
A twilight shade and vista solemn,
  In all these sylvan haunts are found.

And now this fragile garland weaving
  While ebbs the musing tide away,
As one a sacred temple leaving,
  Some tribute on its shrine would lay.

43

I bless the scenes whose tranquil beauty
  Have cheered me like the sense of youth,
And freshened lonely tasks of duty,
  The dream of love and zest of truth.

LOVE AND FAME.

GIVE me the boon of love!
  I ask no more for fame;
Far better one unpurchased heart
  Than glory's proudest name.
Why wake a fever in the blood,
  Or damp the spirit now,
To gain a wreath whose leaves shall wave
  Above a withered brow?

Give me the boon of love!
  Ambition's meed is vain;
Dearer affection's earnest smile
  Than honor's richest train.
I'd rather lean upon a breast
  Responsive to my own,
Than sit pavilioned gorgeously
  Upon a kingly throne.

Like the Chaldean sage,
  Fame's worshippers adore
The brilliant orbs that scatter light
  O'er heaven's azure floor;
But, in their very heart enshrined,
  The votaries of love
Keep e'er the holy flame, which once
  Illumed the courts above.

Give me the boon of love!
  Renown is but a breath,
Whose loudest echo ever floats
  From out the halls of death.
A loving eye beguiles me more
  Than fame's emblazoned seal,
And one sweet note of tenderness
  Than triumph's wildest peal.

Give me the boon of love!
  The path of fame is drear,
And glory's arch doth ever span
  A hill-side cold and sere.
One wild flower from the path of love,
  All lowly though it lie,
Is dearer than the wreath that waves
  To stern ambition's eye.

Give me the boon of love!
  The lamp of fame shines far,
But love's soft light glows near and warm —
  A pure and household star.
One tender glance can fill the soul
  With a perennial fire;
But glory's flame burns fitfully —
  A lone, funereal pyre.

Give me the boon of love!
  Fame's trumpet-strains depart,
But love's sweet lute yields melody
  That lingers in the heart;
And the scroll of fame will burn
  When sea and earth consume,
But the rose of love in a happier sphere
  Will live in deathless bloom.

NEWPORT BEACH.

THE crested line of waves upheaving slow,
Like white-plumed squadrons in compact array,
Moving to launch their thunder on the foe,
Each gathering in, with hushed yet ardent will,
Its strength of purpose ere the war-cloud burst, —
And with accumulate energy press on
Their foamy ridges, to dissolve at last,
Like passion's billows, into gushing tears,
Or, with an inarticulate moan, expire.

Wave after wave successively rolls on
And dies along the shore, until more loud
One billow with concentrate force is heard
To swell prophetic, and exultant rears
A lucent form above its pioneers,
And rushes past them to the farthest goal.
Thus our unuttered feelings rise and fall,
And thought will follow thought in equal waves,

Until reflection nerves design to will,
Or sentiment o'er chance emotion reigns,
And all its wayward undulations blends
In one o'erwhelming surge!

In meditation's hour, these waves recede,
And then appear the relics of the soul—
Trophies long cherished, fragments of wrecked hopes,
That, freshened by the dew of memory, gleam
Like a mosaic pavement, whose dim hues
And worn inscriptions suddenly grow clear
Beneath reviving moisture: purple shells
And gay weeds fleck the strand, like garlands torn
By fierce ambition from the rocks of Time,
To drift unheeded down oblivion's main;
And mystic characters indent the sands
Frail as the records that men love to trace,
With the approaching tide to pass away.

Like the sea, too, our being ebbs and flows
From fountains unexplored of inward life
To the world's sterile coast, with restless dash
Chafing its bound; then mournfully sweeps back
To lapse in earnest consciousness again.
For what to thee, O thoughtful soul, imports
The monotone of apathetic days,

Save as the prelude to a higher strain,
In which the symphony of truth shall blend
With love's celestial anthem? Far apart
From the insensate crowd thy real life,
Like the deep under-current of the sea,
Resistless and invisible flows on:
O, for a human ear attuned to catch
Its muffled voice, or gently beaming eyes
To pierce, with keen regard, the playful wave,
And watch its hidden course!

After each tempest, both of mind and sea,
Cometh tranquillity; then rosy hues
Flush the horizon with a glow that warms
The sleeping flood like Hope's blest reverie,
And the low ripples, with their soothing plash,
Lave the gay-tinted pebbles till they shine
Like precious jewels in the sunset fire;
And the wan moon her slender crescent shows,
A diadem benign, serenely high,
While the lulled wave as gently heaves below
As the fair bosom where is treasured up
Our heart's best life, and its pellucid depths
Reflect the firmament as truthful eyes
With crystal softness mirror love's pure gaze.

What pristine vigor braces the glad frame
That dallies with the breakers, meets the surge,
And feels the sportive tossing of the brine!
As in the world's antagonistic sphere
We wrestle and grow calm, the vague unrest
That haunts impulsive natures, yields awhile
To the encircling presence of the sea,
Inviting thought to an excursive range,
And, with its plaintive or impetuous roar,
Stilling the tumult of the eager heart.

The antique genius shaped a noble truth,
In moulding Aphrodite as she stands
Prepared to yield her beauty to the sea:
A winsome coyness, half made up of fear
And half of love, betrays itself in grace:
With eyes averted from the tempting flood,
She grasps her loosened hair, and as the wave
Strikes her pale feet, a swift recoil
Checks the advancing step, and thus she broods,
A lovely image of subdued desire,
Action and thought, that quiver and unite
In exquisite proportion; thus we pause
Upon the brink of glory unachieved,
Or sacrifice resolved — our hearts appalled
By the chill touch and drear infinitude
Of Fate's relentless tide.

Thy breath, majestic sea, was native air,
And thy cool spray, like Nature's baptism, fell
Upon my brow, while thy hoarse summons called
My childhood's fancy into wonder's realm.
Thy boundless azure in youth's landscape shone
Like a vast talisman, that oft awoke
Visions of distant climes, from weary round
Of irksome life to set my spirit free;
And hence whene'er I greet thy face anew,
Familiar tenderness and awe return
At the wild conjuration; — fondest hopes,
And penitential tears and high resolves
Are born of musing by the solemn deep.

Then here, enfranchised by the voice of God,
O, ponder not, with microscopic eye,
What is adjacent, limited and fixed;
But with high faith gaze forth, and let thy thought
With the illimitable scene expand,
Until the bond of circumstance is rent,
And personal griefs are lost in visions wide
Of an eternal future! Far away
Where looms yon sail, that, like a curlew's wing,
Prints the gray sky, are moored enchanted isles
Of unimagined beauty, with soft airs
And luscious fruitage, and unclouded stars;

Where every breeze wafts music, every path
By flowers o'erhung, leads to a home of love,
And every life is glorified with dreams:
And thus beyond thy present destiny,
Beyond the inlet where the waves of Time
Fret at their barren marge, there spreads a sea
More free and tranquil, where the isles of peace
Shall yield thy highest aspiration scope,
And every sympathy response divine.

THE VESTAL.

A CANADIAN LEGEND.

[A young Chevalier, one of the gallants of the Court of Louis XIV., who, one hundred and fifty years ago, sought glory under the banners of Frontignac, in the wilds of America, is said, by Canadian tradition, to have been tenderly attached to a noble orphan, already destined by her friends and her own pious resolution, to take the veil in the Convent of Montreal. Tradition also says, that, in the simplicity of her heart, she permitted her lover to indulge her in one afternoon's excursion on Lake Champlain, ere she entered the cloister.]

I.

In Life's divine and wondrous song,
  Youth's invocation swells
To Manhood's warfare fierce and vain,
  Which Age serenely tells;
Yet blissful moments intervene,
  Where Eden's glory dwells.

II.

And these the bard should ever strive,
  By numbers sweet and terse,

To consecrate for other souls
  In his melodious verse;
Then list, while I, with humble zeal,
  One episode rehearse.

III.

Two pilgrims—Nature's offspring brave,
  Had roamed the world apart,
And mingled gently with their kind,
  Companionless in heart,
With longings for the unattained,
  In home, and church, and mart.

IV.

The Autumn noon in golden warmth,
  Lay bright on hill and streams,
And round them, like a halo, threw
  Its clear and mellow beams,
Until their spirits seemed to breathe
  The atmosphere of dreams.

V.

Then from between his voice and mind,
  Passed off the chilling spell,
In that mild hour's kind embrace,
  He dared his love to tell;

And trembling words grew softly bold,
  As from his lips they fell.

VI.

There flitted o'er her angel face
  A shade of meek surprise,
And yet the hand was not withdrawn,
  Nor turned aside the eyes;
He felt assurance blest and true
  Within his bosom rise.

VII.

She looked upon the yellow maize,
  With thoughtfulness awhile,
Glanced upward to the peaceful sky,
  Then bent on him a smile,
Whose mournful beauty evermore
  Remembrance will beguile.

VIII.

"As thou dost love me," — every word
  Was stamped upon his brain —
"As thou dost love me, O speak not
  Upon this theme again!
Unless thou wouldst complacently
  Inflict a needless pain.

IX.

"And look not with that tender gaze
So eloquently fond,
Nor murmur those devoted tones,
For on me there's a bond, —
A patient vestal here I wait,
And only hope beyond!

X.

"My path lies up the lonely steep,
O tempt me not below!
Where herbage, air, and sunshine meet
In one transporting glow,
And Life's meandering waters yield
Wild music as they flow.

XI.

"Yet bitter days, methinks, have earned
A right to pluck with tears,
The flower that my rugged way
With God's own promise cheers;
And I will live one hour with thee,
To soothe my coming years.

XII.

"And if there be a future home,
As saintly hearts believe,

Where kindred souls with Freedom crowned,
Earth's destinies retrieve,
By the delight that fills us now,
Thou shalt my troth receive!

XIII.

"Then pledge me by thine eyes of truth,
And brow so nobly fair,
That, having at the fountain drank,
Thou wilt not linger there,
But henceforth silent hasten through
This valley of despair!"

XIV.

Far down upon the tufted shore,
A silver inlet lay,
That winds capriciously along
Until it meets the bay,
And o'er it flocks of blackbirds scream,
And sedges wave alway.

XV.

He led her to a fragile barque
That floated on the tide,
With the same hushed and fearful bliss
That to the altar-side,

When priest and kindred round it stand,
  A lover leads his bride.

XVI.

They nestled in the open stern,
  The moorings off he cast,
And as the green, impending hills
  Seemed drifting slowly past,
They felt the rapture of a mood
  Too heavenly to last.

XVII.

Her head upon his bosom fell,
  Their pulses beat in time,
The balance of their restless hearts,
  Like some exultant chime,
Then won from Earth's discordant tones,
  An interlude sublime.

XVIII.

Now Sympathy's transcendent grace,
  Its latent worth reveals,
He whispered thoughts whose lofty scope
  Truth's inmost fount unseals;
She breathed the music unwares
  That Hope from Memory steals.

XIX.

The lilies bowed their snowy cups
As sped the light wind by,
The scarlet maples flushed around,
And pine-boughs quivered nigh,
While fleecy clouds like sapphire blazed
Athwart the evening sky.

XX.

Their touch, like an enchanter's wand,
Each thrilled with glad alarm,
Their lips were rosy chalices
Yielding delicious balm,
And their pure eyes grew deep and still,
With Love's immortal calm.

XXI.

And as from chaos random stars
Into their orbits roll,
Or weary eagles homeward sweep,
And flutter to their goal,
They felt a holy impulse blend
The senses and the soul.

XXII.

Years have gone by; those pilgrims now
Life's colder rules obey,

60

Thenceforth they met as strangers meet,
  But from that Autumn day,
The thirst of their divided hearts
  Has never passed away.

WASHINGTON'S STATUE.

THE quarry whence thy form majestic sprung
    Has peopled earth with grace,
Heroes and gods that elder bards have sung,
    A bright and peerless race;
But from its sleeping veins ne'er rose before
    A shape of loftier name
Than his, who Glory's wreath with meekness wore,
    The noblest son of Fame.
Sheathed is the sword that Passion never stained;
    His gaze around is cast,
As if the joys of Freedom, newly gained,
    Before his vision passed;
As if a nation's shout of love and pride
    With music filled the air,
And his calm soul was lifted on the tide
    Of deep and grateful prayer;
As if the crystal mirror of his life
    To fancy sweetly came,
With scenes of patient toil and noble strife,
    Undimmed by doubt or shame;

As if the lofty purpose of his soul
    Expression would betray—
The high resolve Ambition to control,
    And trust her crown away!
O, it was well in marble firm and white
    To carve our hero's form,
Whose angel guidance was our strength in fight,
    Our star amid the storm!
Whose matchless truth has made his name divine,
    And human freedom sure,
His country great, his tomb earth's dearest shrine,
    While man and time endure!
And it is well to place his image there,
    Upon the soil he blest;
Let meaner spirits, who its councils share,
    Revere that silent guest!
Let us go up with high and sacred love
    To look on his pure brow,
And as, with solemn grace, he points above,
    Renew the patriot's vow!

TO AN ELM.

Bravely thy old arms fling
Their countless pennons to the fields of air,
And, like a sylvan king,
Their panoply of green still proudly wear.

As some rude tower of old,
Thy massive trunk still rears its rugged form,
With limbs of giant mould,
To battle sternly with the winter's storm.

In Nature's mighty fane,
Thou art the noblest arch beneath the sky ;
How long the pilgrim train
That with a benison have passed thee by!

Lone patriarch of the wood!
Like a true spirit thou dost freely rise,
Of fresh and dauntless mood,
Spreading thy branches to the open skies.

The locust knows thee well,
And when the summer days his notes prolong,
Hid in some leafy cell,
Pours from thy world of green his drowsy song.

Oft, on a morn in spring,
The yellow-bird will seek thy waving spray,
And there securely swing,
To whet his beak, and pour his blithsome lay.

How bursts thy monarch wail,
When sleeps the pulse of Nature's buoyant life,
And, bared to meet the gale,
Wave thy old branches, eager for the strife!

The sunset often weaves
Upon thy crest a wreath of splendor rare,
While the fresh murmuring leaves
Fill with cool sound the evening's sultry air.

Sacred thy roof of green
To rustic dance, and childhood's gambols free,
Gay youth and age serene
Turn with familiar gladness unto thee.

O, hither should we roam,
To hear Truth's herald in the lofty shade;
Beneath thy emerald dome
Might Freedom's champion fitly draw his blade.

With blessings at thy feet,
Falls the worn peasant to his noontide rest;
Thy verdant, calm retreat
Inspires the sad, and soothes the troubled breast.

When, at the twilight hour,
Plays through thy tressil crown the sun's last gleam,
Under thy ancient bower
The schoolboy comes to sport, the bard to dream.

And when the moonbeams fall
Through thy broad canopy upon the grass,
Making a fairy hall,
As o'er the sward the flitting shadows pass;

Then lovers haste to thee,
With hearts that tremble like that shifting light,
To them, O, brave old tree,
Thou art joy's shrine — a temple of delight!

TASSO TO LEONORA.

"That she was aware of his sentiments, and that a mysterious intelligence existed between them, is apparent from the meaning and tendency of innumerable passages scattered through his minor poems — too significant in their application to be mistaken." — *Mrs. Jameson's Loves of the Poets.*

If to love solitude because my heart
  May undisturbed upon thy image dwell,
And in the world to bear a cheerful part
  To hide the fond thoughts that its pulses swell;
If to recall with credulous delight
  Affection's faintest semblance in thee,
To feel thy breath upon my cheek at night,
  And start in anguish that it may not be;
If in thy presence ceaselessly to know
  Delicious peace, a feeling as of wings,
Content divine within my bosom glow,
  A noble scorn of all unworthy things, —
The quiet bliss that fills one's natal air,
  When once again it fans the wanderer's brow,

The conscious spirit of the good and fair—
  The wish to be forever such as now;
If in thy absence still to feel thee nigh,
  Or with impatient longings waste the day,
If to be haunted by thy love-lit eye,
  If for thy good devotedly to pray;
And chiefly sorrow that but half revealed
  Can be the tenderness that in me lies,
That holiest pleasure must be all concealed—
  Shrinking from heartless scoff or base surmise;
If, as my being's crowning grace, to bless
  The hour we recognized each other's truth,
And with calm joy unto my soul confess
  That thou hast realized the dreams of youth,—
My spirit's mate, long cherished, though unknown,
  Friend of my heart bestowed on me by God,
At whose approach all visions else have flown
  From the vain path which I so long have trod;
If from thy sweet caress to bear new life
  As one possessed by a celestial spell,
That armeth me against all outward strife,
  And ever breathes the watchward—all is well;
If with glad firmness, casting doubt aside,
  To bare my heart to thee without disguise,
And yield it up as to my chosen bride,
  Feeling that life vouchsafes no dearer prize;

If thus to blend my very soul with thine
  By mutual consecration, watching o'er
The hallowed bond with loyalty divine —
  If this be love, — I love forevermore!

THE MODERN HERO.

"They also serve who only stand and wait." — MILTON.

THE lance is rusting on the wall,
  No laurel crowns are wove,
And every knightly strain is hushed
  In castle, camp and grove.

No manly breast now fronts the spear,
  No strong arm waves the brand,
To vindicate the rightful cause,
  Or stay Oppression's hand.

The minstrel's pilgrimage has ceased,
  Chivalric days are o'er,
And fiery steeds bear noblemen
  To Palestine no more.

What battle-field with courage now
  Shall ardent minds inspire?
Upon what shrine can youth devote
  Its wild yet hallowed fire?

Must the bold heart ignobly pine
  Far from heroic strife,
And win no trophies to adorn
  This cold and fleeting life ?

Is there no guerdon for the brave ?
  No warfare for the free ?
No wrong for valor to redress ?
  For men no victory ?

Shall high and earnest purpose die,
  And souls of might grow tame ?
Glory no more be warmed to life
  By Love's ennobling flame ?

Forbid it every pulse that leaps
  At Beauty's kindling smile,
Forbid it all the glowing dreams
  That youthful hearts beguile !

By the clear spell that morning weaves,
  By noontide's stirring glare,
By the vast sea, the mighty woods,
  And midnight's solemn air ;

By Nature's deep and constant tones,
  Tears that are born of song,
And thrills that eloquence awakes
  In every human throng;

By childhood's hopefulness serene,
  And woman's cherished name,
Let not heroic spirits yield
  Their heritage of fame!

It may no more be won in arms,
  And knighthood's loyal toil,
Nor flourish, like Marengo's grain,
  Upon a blood-stained soil.

It will not live in warrior's tales,
  Or lay of troubadour,
Nor shall the scarf of ladye-love
  Become its emblem more.

But in the quietude of thought,—
  The soul's divine retreat,
Does Valor now her garlands twine,
  And rear her proudest seat.

They who most bravely can endure,
  Most earnestly pursue,
Amid Opinion's tyrant bands
  Unto themselves be true!

Rejoice in Beauty more than gain,
  Guard well the dreams of youth,
And with devoted firmness live
  Crusaders for the Truth!

The freedom of the mind maintain,
  Its sacredness revere,
And cling to Honor's open path,
  As planets to their sphere;

Who own no gage but that of Faith,
  And with undaunted brow,
Turn from the worshippers of gold,—
  These are the heroes now!

In lonely watchfulness they stand
  Upon Time's hoary steep,
And Glory's flickering beacon-lights,
  For coming ages keep.

Thus bravely live heroic men,
  A consecrated band;
Life is to them a battle-field,
  Their hearts a Holy Land.

HELOISE.

Her beaming look of sweet repose,
  Her mild yet queenly air,
In which a sunny magic glows,
  Luxuriantly fair;
Her soft tones languidly delayed,
  That from such lips are sped,
They seem caressingly afraid
  To leave their rosy bed;
Her laugh that into sparkles breaks
  The listless tide of care,
And to a breezy gladness wakes
  Life's dull and common air;
The spirit of her native wild
  Frank, kindly and sincere,
That, buoyant as a trusting child,
  Lurks in each smile and tear;
Her rich locks, like the warrior's fleece,
  Attracting dews of joy,
Her artless yielding to caprice
  Defying all annoy;

Proclaim that her exultant sail
   To beauty's golden noon,
Has onward swept before the gale
   Of triumph's gay monsoon:
Yet think not as you list and gaze,
   No deeper meaning lies
In the benign and varying rays
   Of those propitious eyes;
No senseless idol of the throng
   Could be so fresh and true,
No cadence of an idle song
   Such lofty dreams renew!

THE GREEK SLAVE.

A STATUE BY POWERS.

Do no human pulses quiver in those wrists that bear
the gyves,
With a noble, sweet endurance, such as moulds heroic
lives?
Is no woman's heart now beating in that bosom's patient
swell?
Do no thoughts of love or glory in that gaze of meek-
ness dwell?

Some pent glow, methinks, diffuses o'er those limbs a
grace of soul,
Warm with Nature, and yet chastened by a holy self-
control;
Teaching how the loyal spirit ne'er can feel an outward
chain,
While its truth remains unconquered, and the will as-
serts her reign.

By the hand that grasps the column, by the foot so calmly press'd,
By the mien sustained though vanquished, and the soft, relying breast—
Light as air may be the fetter that Earth's tyranny doth weave,
And her slaves, by wisest courage, may their destiny retrieve!

By the pride of gentle nurture, unsubdued by freedom's loss,
By the robe so deftly woven, by the locket and the cross—
Half unconscious of thy bondage, on the wings of Faith elate,
Thou art gifted with a being high above thy seeming fate!

What to thee a herd of gazers? what to thee a noisy mart?
Rapt in tranquil, fond seclusion, thou art musing far apart:
As the twilight falls around thee, and thy matchless form I scan,
Rising in serene abstraction, though it wears misfortune's ban;

With thy dimpled arm depending, and thy pure, avert-
ed brow, —
Earnest words I hear thee breathing to thy distant lover
now ; —
Words of triumph, not of wailing, for the cheer of Hope
is thine,
And, immortal in thy beauty, sorrow grows with thee
divine :

"The ark remained while on lone pinion hovered far
the restless dove,
And, though captive, ever o'er me spreads the ægis of
thy love ;
If I could not feel its shielding to the frozen verge of
Time,
If my days were not enlivened with a sense of trust
sublime, —

"Vain the tryst that filled my being, vain the hue that
came and went,
And the vainest of delusions our unspeakable con-
tent !
Let the dream that we have cherished make more dear
each hidden spell,
Quicken every true endeavor, and each baneful image
quell ;

"Give a tone of soulful music to the whisper of the
trees,
Fill the very air with comfort, so that common things
shall please;
Cover with divine inscriptions e'en the lowly-waving
fern,
Make the farthest star in heaven with prophetic radi-
ance burn;

"Draw a sympathetic echo from the plaintive low of
kine,
From the cheerful hum of insects, and the dash of roar-
ing brine;
Meet, full oft, responsive greetings in the twinkle of the
grass,
And the flying cloud's huge shadows, as along the hills
they pass;

"When thy warm lips tremble softly with emotion's
voiceless glow,
And a vague and tender longing makes thy eyelids
overflow —
When thy dark and clustered tresses from the brow are
cast away,
And thy zoneless robe is stirring with the heart's un-
conscious play;

"When a rich and dreamy languor holds thee in a
grateful trance,
As through green and rustling foliage, sky and water
meet thy glance;
Or thy voice spontaneous wanders through some olden
poet's song,
While the hush of deepening twilight all thy fondest
moods prolong;

"When each human accent irks thee like a gossip's
weary tale,
And the idle tricks of Custom make the zest of Nature
stale;
When a lapse of care invites thee momently to summon back,
One by one, the signs of promise that redeem thy
memory's track;

"When a stream or flower charms thee by its beauty's
meek appeal,
Or a magic cadence, quickly, Fancy's sweetest founts
unseal;
When the breeze thy cheek is fanning with the jocund
air of health,
Or before thy sight is waving the full harvest's golden
wealth;

"When to patient self-reliance driven by ungenial things,
All thy lofty spirit broodeth like a bird with drooping wings;
When the depth of this existence awes the flutter of its glee,
In thy struggle and thy quiet, know that I am near to thee!"

ROME.

Roma! Roma! Roma!
Non é piu come era prima.

A TERRACE lifts above the People's square,
Its colonnade;
About it lies the warm and crystal air,
And fir-tree's shade.

Thence a wide scene attracts the patient gaze,
Saint Peter's dome
Looms through the far horizon's purple haze,
Religion's home!

Columns that peer between huge palace walls,
A garden's bloom,
The mount where crumble Cæsar's ivied halls,
The Castle-Tomb;

Egypt's red shaft and Travertine's brown hue,
The moss-grown tiles,
Or the broad firmament of cloudless blue
Our sight beguiles.

Once the awed warrior from yon streamlet's banks
Cast looks benign,
When pointing to his onward-moving ranks,
The holy sign.

Fair women from these casements roses flung
To strew his way,
Who Laura's graces so divinely sung
They live to-day.

In those dim cloisters Palestine's worn bard
His wreath laid by,
Yielding the triumph that his sorrows marred,
Content to die.

From yonder court-yard Beatrice was led,
Whose pictured face
Soft beauty unto sternest anguish wed
In deathless grace.

Here stood Lorraine to watch on many an eve
The sun go down;
There paused Corinne from Oswald to receive
Her fallen crown.

From one imperial trophy turn with pain
The Jews aside,
For on it emblems of their conquered fane
Are still descried.

The mendicant, whose low plea fills thine ear
At every pass,
Before an altar kings have decked, may hear
The chanted mass.

On lofty ceilings vivid frescoes glow,
Auroras beam;
The steeds of Neptune through the water go,
Or Sybils dream.

As in the flickering torchlight shadows weaved
Illusions wild,
Methought Apollo's bosom slightly heaved,
And Juno smiled!

Aerial Mercuries in bronze upspring,
Dianas fly,
And marble Cupids to their Psyches cling,
Without a sigh.

In grottoes, see the hair of Venus[1] creep
    Round dripping stones,
Or thread the endless catacombs where sleep
    Old martyrs' bones.

Upon this esplanade is basking now
    A son of toil,
But not a thought rests on his swarthy brow
    Of Time's vast spoil.

His massive limbs with noblest sculptures vie,
    Devoid of care
Behold him on the sunny terrace lie,
    And drink the air!

With gestures free and looks of eager life,
    Tones deep and mild,
Intent he plies the finger's harmless strife[2]—
    A gleesome child!

The shaggy Calabrese, who lingers near,
    At Christmas comes to play
His reeds before Madonna every year,
    Then hastes away.

[1] The name of a plant.

[2] An Italian peasant's game played with the fingers.

Now mark the rustic pair who dance apart;
What gay surprise!
Her clipsome bodice holds the Roman heart
That lights her eyes:

His rapid steps are timed by native zeal;
The manly chest
Swells with such candid joy that we can feel
Each motion's zest.

What artless pleasure her calm smile betrays,
Whose glances keen
Follow the pastime as she lightly plays
The tambourine!

They know when chestnut groves repast will yield,
Where vineyards spread;
Before their saint at morn they trustful kneeled,
Why doubt or dread?

A bearded Capuchin his cowl throws back,
Demurely nigh;
A Saxon boy with nurse upon his track,
Bounds laughing by.

Still o'er the relics of the Past around
The Day-beams pour,
And winds awake the same continuous sound
They woke of yore.

Thus Nature takes to her embrace serene
What Age has clad,
And all who on her gentle bosom lean
She maketh glad.

TRI-MOUNTAIN.

THROUGH Time's dim atmosphere, behold
  Those ancient hills again,
Rising to Fancy's eager view
  In solitude, as when
Beneath the summer firmament,
  So silently of yore,
The shadow of each passing cloud
  Their rugged bosoms bore!

They sloped in pathless grandeur then
  Down to the murmuring sea,
And rose upon the woodland plain
  In lonely majesty.
The breeze, at noontide, whispered soft
  Their emerald knolls among,
And midnight's wind, amid their heights,
  Its wildest dirges sung.

As on their brow the forest-king
  Paused in his weary way,

From far below his quick ear caught
  The moaning of the bay;
The dry leaves, fanned by autumn's breath,
  Along their ridges crept;
And snow-wreaths, like storm-whitened waves,
  Around them rudely swept.

For ages, o'er their swelling sides,
  Grew the wild flowers of spring,
And stars smiled down, and dew-founts poured
  Their gentle offering.
The moonbeams played upon their peaks,
  And at their feet the tide;
And thus, like altar-mounts, they stood,
  By nature sanctified.

Now, when to mark their beacon-forms
  The seaman turns his gaze,
It quails, as roof, and spire, and dome
  Flash in the sun's bright rays.
On those wild hills a thousand homes
  Are reared in proud array,
And argosies float safely o'er
  That lone and isle-gemmed bay.

Those shadowy mounds, so long untrod,
By countless feet are pressed ;
And hosts of loved ones meekly sleep
Below their teeming breast.
A world's unnumbered voices float
Within their narrow bound;
Love's gentle tone, and traffic's hum,
And music's thrilling sound.

There Liberty first found a tongue
Beneath New England's sky,
And there her earliest martyrs stood,
And nerved themselves to die.
And long upon these ancient hills,
By glory's light enshrined,
May rise the dwellings of the free,
The city of the mind.

THE RINGLET.

The statesman's cabinet was thickly strewn
With parchment scrolls, Ambition's implements:
The hum of passers by, the low, quick note
Of the rich time-piece, the fantastic play
Of chequered light athwart the dusky room,
The sweet aroma and the pensive strain
From his wife's terrace stealing winningly —
Were all unheeded by the man of cares.
You might have known the failure of some aim,
Of more than common import, in the plan
Too intricately wove, of his deep schemes:
For fixed in troubled musings was his gaze,
As restlessly he scanned each lettered roll,
Till thrusting back, in very petulance,
A half-read packet on his cabinet,
The spring-lock of a secret drawer was touched,
And the forgotten nook where, in his youth,
He had been wont to store the treasures small
Of every doting hope, sprang forth unbid;
What mystic token stays his anxious gaze?

And whence that glowing flush? — that mournful
smile?
Ay, and the tear in that world-tutored eye?
List, list! — he speaks — mark well his thoughtful
words;
They may instruct thee, — for men call him great:

"Ringlet of golden hair!
How thou dost move my very manhood now!
Stirring in radiance, there,
As once thou didst above this care-worn brow.

"Methinks it cannot be
That thou art mine; yet, gazing, I do feel
The spell of infancy,
Like distant music, through my bosom steal.

"Sweet relic of that hour!
She who so fondly decked thee, day by day,
As some love-cherished flower,
From the green earth, for aye, has passed away!

"O! what unconscious bliss
Filled this lone breast when thou wert floating free,
Wooing the breeze's kiss!
Symbol of early joy, I welcome thee!

"Would that the sunny hue
That gilds thy silken threads so brightly o'er, —
Would that life's morning dew
Might bathe my restless heart forevermore!

"Unto the spirit-land
Could I, in being's brightness, have been borne, —
Had her fond, trembling hand
From my cold brow this golden ringlet shorn;

"Not, then, should I thus gaze,
And sigh that time has weakened and made dim
The charm which thou dost raise, —
Bright are the tresses of the cherubim!

"Type of life's tranquil spring!
Thy voice is rich and eloquently mild,
The Teacher's echoing:
"'Become thou now e'en as a little child.'"

WINTER.

EARTH in thy cold arms reposes,
  Chilled her bosom's genial glow,
Crystals gleam where blossomed roses,
  Violets long have ceased to blow;
In the bleak air moaning, wave
Leafless branches o'er their grave.

Where the tufted maize once quivered,
  And the vine-stalks lightly curled,
Every golden spear is shivered,
  Every leafy banner furled;
All the fretted landscape shines
With the frost's enamelled lines.

Hushed the voice of singing fountains,
  Woodland strains no longer flow,
And the pine-trees on the mountains,
  Bend beneath their load of snow —
Like stern martyrs waiting doom,
Ready shrouded for the tomb.

All the meadow's grassy billows,
  Lie beneath an ermine shroud,
No green bank the moonbeam pillows,
  When it glances through a cloud;
But the flying drifts look bright,
Sparkling in its silver light.

Downy flakes like dove plumes stealing,
  Stainless robes around have spread,
Earth, the charm of silence feeling,
  Echoes not the muffled tread;
But the chafing breakers wail,
And wild dirges fill the gale.

Stars with keener rays are beaming,
  Through the still and frozen air,
On the ice-bound streamlets gleaming,
  To illume their mute despair —
Heaven's lamps, whose lustre sweet
Glimmers on earth's winding sheet.

While all Nature, thus reposing,
  Yields her charms to winter's sleep,
Let the soul, its buds disclosing,
  Still a spring-like festal keep;
Bid Fancy glean her fruits divine,
And Love his summer garlands twine.

VICTORINE.

She stands all motionless awhile,
The head bowed slightly, as in thought,
Upon the lips a placid smile,
The glance with quiet meaning fraught;
By Heaven! 'tis Judith as she lives
In Guido's nobly-pencilled face,
Made fairer by the spell that gives
A matchless charm to vital grace!

She meekly sits in ardent mood,
With pallid cheek but eye of fire,
Too proud to yield, yet half-subdued
By mournful thought or wild desire;
At once my fancy's wings unfurl
To range a bleak but magic soil,
For as I look upon the girl,
I start to find her Minna Troil!

Her arms are folded on her breast,
  She smiles half scornful, half in glee,
Her eyes are closed, but not in rest,
  You every jetty lash may see ;
There is a zest, a relish high,
  In loveliness thus touched with spite,
Perchance it oftener wakes the sigh,
  But then it makes love's fetters light ;

For none but madmen bow, for life,
  To beauty which is lapped in pride,
That coldly mocks affection's strife,
  And yields not to devotion's tide ;
Yet who would shrink from such a fate
  With scorn so lovely ever nigh ?
The very look of shrewish Kate,
  The very air of Lady Di !

Methinks thou frownest at my lay ;
  O would that I were there to see !
"The hateful man" — I hear thee say —
  "To write such saucy things of me !"
Well, little Cleopatra, now
  I will not trace thy picture more,
I'll leave thy lip and cheek and brow
  For sweeter minstrels to explore ;

But for those windows of the soul—
  Those eyes in which 'tis heaven to dwell,
The stars of fate, hope's brightest goal,
  Methinks I know their language well;
And were the fairy's powers mine,
  I'd watch beside thy couch to-night,
And on them squeeze the flower divine
  That makes the dreamer love at sight!

IL PENSEROSO.

Are we not exiles here?
Come there not o'er us memories of a clime
More genial and more dear
Than this of time?

When deep, vague wishes press
Upon the soul and prompt it to aspire,
A mystic loneliness,
And wild desire;

When our long-baffled zeal
Turns back, in mockery, on the weary heart,
Till at the sad appeal,
Dismayed we start;

And like the Deluge dove,
Outflown upon the world's cold sea we lie,
And all our dreams of love
In anguish die:

Nature no more endears,
Her blissful strains seem only breathed afar,
Nor mount, nor flower cheers,
Nor smiling star:

Familiar things grow strange,
Fond hopes, like tendrils shooting to the air,
Through friendless being range,
To meet despair:

And nursed by secret tears,
Rich but frail visions in the heart have birth,
And this fair world appears
A homeless earth!

Then must we summon back
Blest guides who long ago have met the strife,
And left a radiant track
To mark their life;

Then must we look around
On heroes' deeds — the landmarks of the brave,
And hear their cheers resound
From off the wave;

Then must we turn from show,
Pleasure and fame, the phantom race of care,
And let our spirits flow
In earnest prayer!

SLEEPY HOLLOW.

Beneath these gold and azure skies,
  The river winds through leafy glades,
Save where, like battlements, arise
  The gray and tufted palisades.

The fervor of this sultry time
  Is tempered by the humid earth,
And zephyrs born of summer's prime,
  Give a delicious coolness birth.

They freshen this sequestered nook
  With constant greetings bland and free;
The pages of the open book
  All flutter with their wayward glee.

As quicker swell their breathings soft,
  Cloud shadows skim along the field;
And yonder dangling woodbines oft
  Their crimson bugles gently yield.

The tulip tree majestic stirs,
  Far down the water's marge beside,
And now awake the nearer firs,
  And toss their ample branches wide.

How blithely trails the pendent vine!
  The grain slope lies in green repose;
Through the dark foliage of the pine
  And lofty elms, the sunshine glows.

Like sentinels in firm array
  The trees of life their shafts uprear;
Red cones upon the sumac play,
  And ancient locusts whisper near.

From wave and meadow, cliff and sky,
  Let thy stray vision homeward fall;
Behold the mist-bloom floating nigh,
  And hollyhock white-edged and tall;

Its gaudy leaves, though fanned apart,
  Round thick and mealy stamens spring,
And nestled to its crimson heart,
  The sated bees enamored cling.

Mark the broad terrace flecked with light,
  That peeps through trellises of rose,
And quivers with a vague delight,
  As each pale shadow comes and goes.

The near, low gurgle of the brook,
  The wren's glad chirp, the scented hay,
And e'en the watch-dog's peaceful look
  Our vain disquietudes allay.

O, were our lives attuned to glide,
  Like this serene and balmy day,
Might we arrest its radiant tide,
  And breathe its tranquil joy alway ;

Or were our prisoned hearts to know
  The freedom of this cheering air,
And, like this sunshine, ever glow,
  Undimmed by doubt, or fear or care ;

Fond glances e'er would light the eye,
  Smiles wreathe the lip, peace crown the brow,
For the content would never die
  That can but live in memory now !

LORD BYRON AT VENICE.

A SAFFRON tint o'erspread the broad lagoon
Caught from the golden west, and as its flush
Deepened to crimson, and the crystal air
Beamed like a rainbow, sweetly was revealed
The secret of their art, whose magic hues
Still make the palace walls of Venice glow
With colors born in heaven.
Men of all climes
Cluster within her square — the passive Turk,
With jewelled turban, the mercurial Greek,
And sombre Jew, and, gliding with a step
Whose echo stirs the heart, fair shapes flit by,
Shrouded in black; yet evening wakes not there
The sounds that fill the cities of the land;
No rumbling wheel or tramp of passing steed
Drowns the low hum of voices as they rise;
But from her window, on a lone canal,
The fair Venetian hears the plash of oars,
The tide that ripples by the mossy wall,

Some distant melody or convent bell,
And cry of gondoliers, when their bright prows
Clash at an angle of the lonely street.
From the deep shadow of the Ducal pile
Shot a dark barge, that floated gently on
Into the bosom of the quiet bay;
And springing lightly thence, a noble form
Revelled alone amid the sleeping waves;
Now, like an athlete, cleaving swift his way,
And now, the image of a sculptor's dream,
Pillowed upon the sea, gazing entranced
From that wild couch up to the rosy clouds;
And cradled thus, like her whom he adored,
Beauty's immortal goddess, at her birth,
His throbbing brow grew still, and his whole frame
Nerved with refreshing coolness, and the thirst
Of passion's fever vanished from his heart;
He turned from Venice, with a bitter smile,
To the vast firmament and waters pure,
And, eager for their clear tranquillity,
Sighed for a home in some far nook of earth,
Where to one true and genial soul allied,
His restless spirit might be fed with hope,
Till peace should steal upon him, like the calm
Of that delicious eve!

LUNA.—AN ODE.

THE south wind hath its balm, the sea its cheer,
And autumn woods their bright and myriad hues;
Thine is a joy that love and faith endear,
And awe subdues:
The wave-tost seamen and the harvest crew,
When on their golden sheaves the quivering dew
Hangs like pure tears—all fear beguile,
In glancing from their task to thy maternal smile!
The mist of hill-tops undulating wreathes,
At thy enchanting touch, a magic woof,
And curling incense fainter odor breathes,
And, in transparent clouds, hangs round the vaulted roof.
Huge icebergs, with their crystal spires,
Slow heaving from the northern main,
Like frozen monuments of high desires
Destined to melt in nothingness again,—
Float in thy mystic beams,
As piles aerial down the tide of dreams!

A sacred greeting falls
With thy mild presence, on the ruined fane,
Columns time-stained, dim frieze, and ivied walls,
As if a fond delight thou didst attain
To mingle with the Past,
And o'er her trophies lone a holy mantle cast!
Along the billow's snowy crest
Thy beams a moment rest,
And then, in sparkling mirth, dissolve away ;
Through forest boughs, amid the withered leaves,
Thy light a tracery weaves,
And on the mossy clumps its rays fantastic play.
With thee, ethereal guide,
What reverent joy to pace the temple floor,
And watch thy silver tide
O'er statue, tomb and arch its solemn radiance pour!
Like a celestial magnet thou dost sway
The untamed waters in their ebb and flow,
The maniac raves beneath thy pallid ray,
And poet's visions glow.
Madonna of the stars! through the cold prison-grate
Thou stealest, like a nun on mercy bent,
To cheer the desolate,
And usher in grief's tears when her mute pang is spent!
I marvel not that once thy altars rose
Sacred to human woes,

And nations deemed thee arbitress of Fate,
To whom enamored virgins made their prayer,
Or widows in their first despair,
And wistful gazed upon thy queenly state,
As, with a meek assurance, gliding by,
In might and beauty unelate,
Into the bridal chambers of the sky!
And less I marvel that Endymion sighed
To yield his spirit unto thine,
And felt thee soul-allied,
Making his being thy receptive shrine.
A lofty peace is thine; — the tides of life
Flow gently when thy soothing orb appears,
And passion's fevered strife
From thy chaste glow imbibes the calmness of the spheres.
O twilight glory! that doth ne'er awake
Exhausting joy, but evenly and fond,
Allays the immortal thirst it cannot slake,
And heals the chafing of the work-day bond;
Give me thy patient spell! — to bear
With an unclouded brow, the secret pain,
(That floods my soul as thy pale beams the air,)
Of hopes that Reason quells, for Love to wake again!

EVA.

O not with heartless eulogy, or flattery's idle word,
Can I approach the crystal fount God's breath has often stirred;
With thee I own a higher spell, and feel a purer air,
For when I strive to speak thy praise, it trembles into prayer!
Prophetic thoughts that silent dwell beside the source of tears,
And hopes that seem too sweet and high to know the blight of years, —
A solemn tenderness that pleads that life to such as thee
May prove more happy and divine than it is wont to be, —
All — all forbid that I profane the shrine of grace and youth,
With any tribute but a wreath twined by the hand of truth.

As I listen to thy gentle voice, and look within thine eyes,
To trace the workings of thy soul with exquisite surprise,
Or watch thy fancies quiver like dew-drops on the grass,
I think some dream of beauty in thee has come to pass;
And visions rise of fairer worlds whose memory time has quelled,
The weight of life is lifted, the gloom of earth dispelled;
I see the bloom upon the grass, the sparkle on the wave,
And fear no more the shaft of fate, or shadow of the grave;
A faith in something bright and good that cannot pass away,
Redeems the world from loneliness and hope from slow decay.
I ask not for thee, dearest, the weary crown of fame,
Earth boasts no sweeter title than thy loved and gentle name;
I would not that thy goodness should dim in fortune's glare,
Or thy flowers of pleasure wither in the world's corrupted air;

But round thy pathway ever may kindly spirits throng,
And thy soul ne'er vainly listen for an echo to her song;
And when affection's vine shall shoot around its elm to
twine,
O mayst thou find as fond a heart and true a love as
mine!

TO LADY BLANCHE:

A FAVORITE STEED.

O gentle steed! ere thou dost go,
Let pleasant memories overflow,
To speak thy just renown;
For who unmoved can thee behold,
Thy spotless coat, thy graceful mould,
And rich mane floating down?

As thus I pat thy neck of snow,
Delicious fancies come and go,
Like thy soft eye's dilating;
Thou callest back the days of yore,
When Faith's emprize Love's guerdon wore,
Heroic deeds creating.

I think how rarely blend in thee
High spirit and docility,
Good faith and playful art;

How, moving as the reins direct,
Thou dost such nonchalance affect —
A woman's counterpart!

For, while sequestered paths beside
Thy dainty feet right onward glide,
Unconscious speed betraying;
Let but spectators come in view,
Thou dost each winsome trick renew,
Thine every grace displaying!

Yet one blest truth from this I draw,
And trace in thy caprice a law
That lends new worth to beauty;
High instincts mannered charms impart
But for the chosen of the heart
Still keep all love and duty.

On such a steed sprung Lochinvar,
To bear so gallantly afar
The maid he bravely wooed;
On such a steed the martyr-queen,
Bewildered, tearful, yet serene,
Passed on to Holyrood.

Of all thy praise be this the meed,
No attribute can this exceed,
  Thou doest the behest
Of one who finds in thee a throne,
As firm and cheering as her own
  In hearts where she 's a guest.

Then arch thy neck with noble zeal,
Her hand upon thy mane to feel,
  And leap, curvet and prance!
Amble! — we have a word to say —
Fly! — how life's wings exultant play!
  Hurrah for Lady Blanche!

SURREY TO GERALDINE.

"She was so beautiful as to authorize the raptures of her poetical lover; and too proud of such a suitor to let him escape. He betrays an indignant consciousness of the arts by which she keeps him entangled in her chain; and accuses her expressly of a love of general admiration, and of giving her countenance and favor to unworthy rivals."—*Mrs. Jameson's Loves of the Poets.*

ALONE once more!—but with such deep emotion,
Waking to life a thousand hopes and fears,
Such wild distrust—such absolute devotion,
My bosom seems a dreary lake of tears;—

Tears that stern manhood long restrained from gushing,
As mountains keep a river from the sea,
Until spring's floods impetuously rushing,
Channel a bed, and set its waters free!

What mockery to all true and earnest feeling,
This fatal union of the false and fair!
Eyes, lips, and voice unmeasured bliss revealing,
With hearts whose lightness fills us with despair!

Oh God! some sorrows of our wondrous being,
  A patient mind can partly clear away;
Ambition cools when fortune's gifts are fleeing,
  And men grow thoughtful round a brother's clay;—

But to what end this waste of noble passion?
  This wearing of a truthful heart to dust—
Adoring slaves of humor, praise, or fashion,
  The vain recipients of a boundless trust?

Come home, fond heart, cease all instinctive pleading,
  As the dread fever of insane desire,
To some dark gulf thy warm affections leading,
  When love must long survive, though faith expire!

Though wonted glory from the earth will vanish,
  And life seem desolate and hope beguile,
Love's cherished dream learn steadfastly to banish,
  Till death thy spirit's conflict reconcile!

WEST POINT.

Wild umbrage far around me clings
  To breezy knoll and hushed ravine,
And o'er each rocky headland flings
  Its mantle of refreshing green.

The echoes that so boldly rung
  When cannon flashed from steep to steep,
And Freedom's airy challenge flung,
  In each romantic valley sleep.

His counsels here our chieftain breathed,
  Here roved his mild, undaunted eye,
When yon lone fort with thickets wreathed,
  Held captive Britain's gallant spy.

Fit home to rear a nation's youth
  By self-control to nerve the will,
Through knowledge gain expansive truth,
  And with high aims life's circle fill.

How grateful is the sudden change
  From arid pavements to the grass,
From narrow streets that thousands range,
  To meadows where June's zephyrs pass !

Beneath the cliffs the river steals
  In darksome eddies to the shore,
But midway every sail reveals
  Reflected on its crystal floor.

In tranquil mood the cattle walk
  Along the verdant marge to feed,
While poised upon the mullein stalk
  The chirping red-bird picks the seed.

Low murmurs in the foliage bred,
  The clear horizon's azure line,
Fresh turf elastic to the tread,
  And leafy canopies are thine.

White fleecy clouds move slowly by,
  How cool their shadows fall to-day !
A moment on the hills they lie,
  And then like spirits glide away.

Amid the herbage, yesternight,
His web the cunning spider threw,
And now, as sparkling diamonds bright,
It glistens with the pendent dew.

Gay butterflies dart on and sink
O'er the sweet blossoms of the pea,
And from the clover's globe of pink
Contented hums the downy bee.

In all this varied beauty glows
Deep meaning for the thoughtful heart,
As it were fain to teach repose,
And lofty confidence impart.

How vivid to my fancy now,
Uprise the forms that life redeem !
The ardent eye — the open brow,
And tender smile beside me seem.

For Nature's presence gathers back
The deeds that grace, the loves that cheer,
And as her holy steps we track,
Hope's rainbow breaks through sorrow's tear.

THE DIRGE OF THE MARINER.

I ASK not to sleep where the ancient church bell
   Its echoes will ring o'er my grave,
More dear than its chime is the requiem swell
   And musical moan of the wave :
Let not the frail herbage grow over my bones
   Which the winter gales cover with snow,
O bury me not where memorial stones
   Earth's chronicled sepulchres show !

But place me away where the curlews sweep
   Round the ocean's unlaurelled goal,
On the sparkling beach where the surges sleep,
   And crags the tide control ;
I have lived on its mighty and solemn breast,
   And I love it far more than land,
O, when I am dead, let my ashes rest
   Entombed on the desolate strand !

For there the green billows with chaplets of foam,
   Will come from the midst of the sea,

Like friends from the haunts of my olden home,
   To utter their sorrow for me;
They will bring gay weeds from the fathomless caves
   And twine them above my head,
And the ambient gleam of the playful waves
   They'll cast on my peaceful bed:

And shells like the rainbow, with pebbles rare,
   They'll strew on the lonely strand,
While the signs of their faithful vigils there
   Will be traced on the glistening sand:
Sadly the sound of their mournful retreat
   In the distance will die away,
And wildly the sobs of their coming will greet
   The home of the mariner's clay.

They'll haste on the wings of the tempest to wail,
   Or under the starlight to sigh,
They'll throng like an army its chieftain to hail,
   Or meekly creep thither to die;
Let my slab be inscribed by the radiant wave,
   My shroud be enwove from the surge,
Let no tears but the spray wet the mariner's grave,
   And the sea breathe forever his dirge!

THE NIGHT-BLOOMING CEREUS.

How coyly thou the golden hours dost number!
  Not all their splendor can thy love beguile;
Vainly the morning zephyrs fan thy slumber,
  And noon's rich glory wooes thee for a smile.

For thou dost blossom when cool shadows hover,
  And dews are falling through the dusky air;
When with new fervor dreams the happy lover,
  And winds grow solemn with the voice of prayer.

While all around thee earth's bright things are sleeping,
  Gay lilies fade and droops the crimson rose,
Fresh is the vigil thou alone art keeping,
  And sweet the charms thy virgin leaves disclose.

Thus, in the soul, is deep love ever hidden,
  Thus noble minds will fondly shun the throng,
And, at their chosen time, start forth unbidden,
  With peerless valor or undying song.

Thus the true heart its mystic leaves concealing,
  Folds them serenely from the world's broad glare,
Its treasured bliss and inmost grief revealing
  To the calm starlight and the dewy air.

Blest is thy lesson, vestal of the flowers, —
  Not in the sunshine is our whole delight ;
Some joys bloom only in life's pensive hours,
  And pour their fragrance on the breeze of night.

THE HOLY LAND.

THROUGH the warm noontide, I have roamed
Where Cæsar's palace-ruins lie,
And in the Forum's lonely waste,
Oft listened to the night-wind's sigh.

I've traced the moss-lines on the walls
That Venice conjured from the sea,
And seen the Coliseum's dust
Before the breeze of autumn flee.

Along Pompeii's lava-street,
With curious eye, I've wandered lone,
And marked Segesta's temple-floor
With the rank weeds of ages grown.

I've clambered Ætna's hoary brow,
And sought the wild Campagna's gloom,
I've hailed Geneva's azure tide,
And snatched a weed from Virgil's tomb.

Why all unsated yearns my heart
To seek once more a Pilgrim shrine?
One other land I would explore,—
The sacred fields of Palestine.

Oh, for a glance at those wild hills,
That round Jerusalem arise!
And one sweet evening by the lake
That gleams beneath Judea's skies!

How anthem-like the wind must sound
In meadows of the Holy Land,
How musical the ripples break
Upon the Jordan's moonlit strand!

Behold the dew, like angels' tears,
Upon each thorn is gleaming now,
Blest emblem of the crown of love
There woven for the sufferer's brow.

Who does not sigh to enter Nain,
Or in Capernaum to dwell;
Inhale the breeze from Galilee,
And rest beside Samaria's well?

Who would not stand beneath the spot
Where Bethlehem's star its vigil kept?
List to the plash of Siloa's pool,
And kiss the ground where Jesus wept?

Gethsemane who would not seek,
And pluck a lily by the way?
Through Bethany devoutly walk,
And on the Mount of Olives pray?

How dear were one repentant night
Where Mary's tears of love were shed!
How blest beside the Saviour's tomb,
One hour's communion with the dead!

What solemn joy to stand alone
On Calvary's celestial height!
Or kneel upon the mountain-slope,
Once radiant with supernal light!

I cannot throw my staff aside,
Nor wholly quell the hope divine,
That one delight awaits me yet, —
A pilgrimage to Palestine.

LOVE AND TIME.

Let those lament thy flight,
Who find a new delight
In every hour that o'er them swiftly flies;
Whose hearts are free and strong
As some well-carolled song,
That charms the ear with ever fresh surprise.

To Wealth's stern devotee
Too fast the moments flee,
That gainful schemes to golden issues bring;
And Fame's deluded child,
By Glory's dream beguiled,
To twine his laurel wreath would stay thy wing.

They who have learned to bind
The warm and restless mind
In soft content to Pleasure's rosy car,
May sigh to hold thee back,
And linger on the track
That sends no lofty promise from afar.

But by the heart that turns
To those celestial urns
That with Love's dew forever overflow,
Uncherished are the years
No sympathy endears,
When all thy flowers droop beneath the snow.

What holy spell is thine
To bless a lonely shrine,
Or wake glad echoes where no music flows?
Why to a barren thing
With senseless ardor cling,
Or gardens till that never yield a rose?

Yet when devotion pure
Breeds courage to endure,
And grace to hallow the career of time,
When for another's joy
Thy moments we employ,
Like clouds by sunbeams lit, they grow sublime.

The tender, true and brave
Disdain a gift to save
In which self only claims a weary part;
Nor would thy course delay
To pamper their frail clay,
And life consume in tricks of soulless art.

Haste, then, till thou hast brought
The good so fondly sought,
And Love's bright harvest richly waves at last!
Then will I call thee mine,
And hail thee as divine,
The present cherish, nor lament the past.

THE TWO PALMS.

As the last column of a temple vanished,
   A Palm-tree, in a city of the West,
Stood, like a hero from his country banished,
   A proud though lonely guest.

Perchance its birthplace was a holy mountain,
   Or radiant valley of some tropic isle,
Near pyramid, or mosque, or wayside fountain,
   By Jordan or the Nile.

And oft its high and tufted crest beholding,
   In each vibration of the arching leaves,
A plaintive strain I seemed to hear unfolding,
   As when an exile grieves.

For solemn is the air of isolation,
   And that lone offspring of the desert wild,
Wore to my eye a look of consecration,
   That sympathy beguiled.

No more around it eastern balms were stealing,
  But smoke and dingy vapors of the town,
No Moslem in its pillared shade was kneeling,
  Nor caravan sunk down.

Before it once the sandy ridges heaving,
  Spread like an ocean, limitless and free,
And the mirage its panorama weaving,
  Rose beautiful to see!

Now waves of eager life beneath it swelling,
  With restless care mock oriental ease,
And chimney-stacks, tiled roof and murky dwelling,
  Shut out the sun and breeze.

Yet even here I marked, each day, appearing
  An aged Syrian, sorrowful and calm,
With folded arms, wan smile, and looks endearing
  Cast on the lonely Palm.

And once he murmured, as the night descended,
  While gazing fondly through unconscious tears,
"Fair tree, the promise of thy life is ended,
  For here thou hast no peers."

How near the good we distantly are craving!
  The Syrian long had weary vigil kept;
One morn his country's tree was gaily waving,
  It blossomed while he slept!

Some far-off nook of that vast city treasured
  Another Palm by careless eyes unseen,
That drearily the lingering years had measured,
  Yet put forth shoots of green;

Until its ripened flower-dust uplifting,
  On the stray currents of the tideless air,
With certain aim to this pent garden drifting,
  A mate encountered there!

Thus seeds of truth their noiseless flight are winging
  And love instinctively steals through the crowd,
To hearts receptive consolation bringing,
  They may not breathe aloud!

Accept the omen, thou who toilest lonely,
  And patiently Life's blossoming await;
Where God has planted thee be faithful only,
  And thou shalt conquer Fate!

THE UNKNOWN PORTRAIT.

In an old palace by the Arno's side,
 Rich in sweet wonders of the rainbow art,
One portrait, with a look of gentle pride,
 Seems to invoke the gazer's eye and heart.

Dark plumes his broad and manly forehead shade,
 And in his grasp a jewelled hilt appears;
Some dream of hope before him seems to fade,
 And youth to wear the thoughtfulness of years.

For ardent purpose, in that noble face,
 Is tempered by a mild reflective mood;
The soldier's pride blends with the poet's grace,
 And love o'er courage dove-like seems to brood.

His race was high — I see it written now,
 In the knight's weapon and the princely dress;
And more than all in the uplifted brow,
 The stately air, and smile of gentleness.

He was a hero — though, perchance, his deeds
  Fame's partial glance swept all unheeded by ;
The clear resolve of valor warmly pleads
  For honor's garland in his dauntless eye.

He must have loved — I know it by the thought
  That o'er his youthful bloom a shade hath cast,
Like the sweet twilight, with calm sadness fraught,
  That lingers when the sultry day is past.

Methinks some being fair, with love's keen gaze,
  Watched o'er the limner as these lines he traced ;
Time dimmed their hues, but grief nor length of days
  The magic semblance from her soul effaced.

O frail memorial of the young and brave,
  Vain trophy of a human brother's lot,
No record from oblivion thou dost save,
  But that he lived, and loved, and is forgot !

TO THE CYPRESS.

Slow-waving Cypress of the land of song!
Perennial mourner! — though thou art
Amid the glories of the sylvan throng,
Most eloquent of sadness to the heart;
Yet ever welcome to the weary eye,
Thy graceful shaft of foliated green,
Against the azure of the morning sky,
Upreared in beauty, solemn and serene.
And where afar Day's vesper beacons blaze
Upon Fiesole or Mario's height,
Touching with flame each mountain altar round,
Shed on thy verdant cones a rosy gleam,
And winds among thy boughs a requiem sound,
What fitting cenotaphs for man ye seem!

LAKE CANEPO.

WHEN cradled on thy placid breast,
   In hushed content I loved to muse,
Too full the heart, too sweet the rest
   For thought and speech to interfuse.

But now, when thou art shrined afar,
   Like Nature's chosen urn of peace,
Remembrance, like the evening star,
   Begins a vigil ne'er to cease.

Each mossy rock, each fairy isle,
   Inlets with thickets overhung,
The cloud's rose-tint or fleecy pile,
   And Echo's wildly-frolic tongue;

The light and shade that o'er thee play,
   The ripple of thy moonlit wave,
The long, calm, dreamy summer day,
   The very stones thy waters lave;

The converse frank, the harmless jest,
  The reverie without a sigh,
The hammock's undulating rest,
  With fair companions seated by ;

Yet linger, as if near thee still,
  I heard, upon the fitful breeze,
The locust and the whippoorwill,
  Or rustle of the swaying trees.

Hills rise in graceful curves around,
  Here dark with tangled forest shade,
There yellow with the harvest-ground,
  Or emerald with the open glade ;

Primeval chestnuts line the strand,
  And hemlocks every mountain side,
While, by each passing zephyr fanned,
  Azalia flowers kiss the tide.

We nestle in the gliding barge,
  And turn from yon unclouded sky,
To watch, along the bosky marge,
  Its image in thy waters nigh.

Or, gently darting to and fro,
  The insects on their face explore,
With speckled minnows poised below,
  And tortoise on the pebbly floor.

Or turn the prow to some lone bay,
  Where thick the floating leaves are spread ;
How bright and queen-like the array
  Of lilies in their crystal bed !

Like chalices for beauty's lip
  Their snowy cones half open lie,
The dewdrops of the morn to sip,
  But close to day's intrusive eye.

And in their pure and stately grace,
  Their shrinking from the noontide glare,
The charm they yield their dwelling-place,
  How like the noblest of the fair !

To thy serene and balmy air,
  Above life's vain and common things,
Should gentle spirits oft repair,
  And fondly plume their drooping wings.

O let me thence, in fancy, bear
  The dreams of youth by thee renewed;
And hallow the domain of care
  With visions born in solitude.

FAITH'S WARNING.

THE vital elements of all things gifted
With promise or with truth,
By God's own hand benignantly are lifted
Into perennial youth.

O then, with gentle reverence, surrender
The wish to interfere,
Behold the miracle, devout and tender,
But enter not its sphere!

Childhood, with meek intelligence, appealing,
When guardians annoy,
As gush the sympathies its life revealing,
Asks freedom to enjoy.

Genius, by graceful waywardness, achieving
Its claim the boon to share,
A narrow doom in Fancy's world retrieving,
Expands untrammelled there.

The throes of nations plead that right be tested—
The Present grapple fairly with the Past,
For Liberty's pure zeal, if unmolested,
Will triumph at the last!

Profane not Love in its divine seclusion,
If true, its hope is sure ;
Born in weak hearts it is a chance illusion,
That vainly would endure.

For all things destined to survive, engender
Their own progressive life,
And Truth forsaken by her last defender,
Yet conquers in the strife.

In its dim crypt of mould the seed implanted
Will germinate and spring ;
Poised in her azure realm, the lark undaunted
Exultingly will sing.

The prayer of wisdom, in these later ages,
Is for unchartered right
To turn, at will, her own elected pages,
With unimpeded sight.

To their own law abandon all things real,
Nor, with incessant care,
Strive to conform to thy perverse ideal
What God created fair.

SONNETS.

SONNETS.

I.

FREEDOM.

Freedom! beneath thy banner I was born,
  Oh let me share thy full and perfect life!
Teach me opinion's slavery to scorn,
  And to be free from passion's bitter strife;
Free of the world, a self-dependent soul,
  Nourished by lofty aims and genial truth,
And made more free by love's serene control,
  The spell of beauty and the hopes of youth.
The liberty of nature let me know,
  Caught from tho mountains, groves and crystal
      streams;
Her starry host, and sunset's purple glow,
  That woo the spirit with celestial dreams,
On fancy's wing exultingly to soar,
Till life's harsh fetters clog the heart no more.!

II.

VANDERLYN'S ARIADNE.

How like a vision of pure love she seems!
Her cheek just flushed with innocent repose,
That folds her thoughts up in delicious dreams,
Like dewdrops in the chalice of a rose;
Pillowed upon her arm and raven hair,
How archly rests that bright and peaceful brow!
Its rounded pearl defiance bids to care,
While kisses on the lips seem melting now;
Prone in unconscious loveliness she lies,
And leaves around her delicately sway;
Veiled is the splendor of her beaming eyes,
But o'er the limbs bewitching graces play:
Ere into Eden's groves the serpent crept,
Thus Eve within her leafy arbor slept.

III.

TO ONE DECEIVED.

All hearts are not disloyal; let thy trust
Be deep and clear and all-confiding still,
For though Love's fruit turn on the lips to dust,
She ne'er betrays her child to lasting ill:
Through leagues of desert must the pilgrim go
Ere on his gaze the holy turrets rise;
Through the long sultry day the stream must flow
Ere it can mirror twilight's purple skies.
Fall back unscathed from contact with the vain,
Keep thy robes white, thy spirit bold and free,
And calmly launch affection's barque again,
Hopeful of golden spoils reserved for thee;
Though lone the way as that already trod,
Cling to thine own integrity and God!

IV.

SLEEP.

SWEETEST of mysteries! — thy dews revive
  Hearts that seemed blighted by toil's wasting rime;
They start from thy embrace again to strive,
  And with new ardor breast the surge of time.
Blest interlude! whose music conquers care,
  Maternal sleep, how soon away from thee
Does life her young enchantments vainly wear,
  And all our sense of pleasure cease to be!
Thou art the angel that doth come at night
  To set us free, as was the saint of yore;
The blessing that doth crown us for the fight,
  The fount perennial on a barren shore:
Thine is the gift of dreams, the trance of love,
And in thy breast peace nestles like a dove.

V.

THE WILLOW.

As o'er thy pendent leaves the zephyr flies,
Lifting their silver lining to the light,
Their mournful shiver, like a thousand sighs,
Wakes in the heart a tremulous delight.
Thy weeping vigil consecrates the grave,
When through each trailing bough the moonshine gleams,
And, like hopes cast upon oblivion's wave,
Thy withered verdure flecks the autumn streams.
What graceful meekness sways thy drooping form,
Thou sylvan effigy of love and wo!
In gentle patience yielding to the storm,
The wisdom of a lowly trust to show:
Of thee divinely sung Othello's bride,
And in thy shade the fair Ophelia died.

VI.

THE BALCONY.

Rare was the pastime o'er thy rail to lean,
  And gaze upon the motley crowd below,
Or trace the distant valleys broad and green,
  Girded by hills whose tops were bright with snow:
It was a spot to muse: — life's waters beat
  Like a swift river in tumultuous flow,
Winding capriciously beneath my feet,
  While flushed its wave with nature's purest glow.
But when around night's balmy silence fell,
  Thou wert a paradise, for by my side
Stood one, whose presence, like a grateful spell,
  That scene of tranquil beauty glorified:
And now thy name wakes thoughts of love that seem
Like the remembered music of a dream!

VII.

ON A LANDSCAPE BY BACKHUYSEN.

Not for the eye alone are here outspread
  Skies, fields, and herds in such divine repose;
The soul of beauty that to these is wed,
  Through the fair landscape tremulously glows!
We seem to feel the meadow's grateful air,
  Hear the low breathing of the dreamy kine,
And the pure fragrance of the harvest share,
  Until our hearts all cold distrust resign,
Feeling once more to truth and love allied;
  And, while the rich tranquillity we view,
Each good they have foretold and life denied,
  Hope's sweetest promises again renew,
As if the twilight angel hovered there,
To waft from nature's rest a balm for human care.

VIII.

THE INDIAN SUMMER.

THE few sere leaves that to the branches cling,
Fall not to-day, so light the zephyr's breath ;
O'er Autumn's sleep now plays the breeze of Spring,
Like love's warm kiss upon the brow of death :
Serene the firmament, save where a haze
Of dreamy softness floats upon the air,
Or a bright cloud of amber seems to gaze
In mild surprise upon the meadows bare :
Summer revives, and, like a tender strain
Borne on the night-breeze to the wondering ear,
With tender sighs melts Winter's frosty chain,
And smiles once more upon the dying year :
Thus when we deem Time's frost has chilled the heart,
At Love's sweet call its languid pulses start.

IX.

ON A PORTRAIT OF MRS. NORTON.

Oh, who can meet those dark and liquid eyes,
And see that form so queenlike in its grace,
Nor feel a thrill of passionate surprise
That men could mingle shame with such a face?
Did they behold thee who the slander nursed?
Communed they ever with thy tender lays?
And felt they not their very manhood cursed
Beneath thine earnest and bewildering gaze?
Sweetness and pride that unto truth belong,
Through every lineament divinely steal,
And like the cadence of thy gentle song,
Pure and devoted sympathies reveal:
O radiant minstrel! Let it solace thee
That thou art warmly loved beyond the sea!

X.

ON A BUST OF WEBSTER.

There is a Roman grandeur in that brow,
  And lofty thoughts within it seem enshrined,
As calmly it expands before me now,
  Nature's assurance of a noble mind;
A stern serenity broods o'er the face,
  Most eloquent of a determined soul,
Will softened by the lines of mental grace,
  Yet firm of purpose, strong in self-control:
How glorious the art that can subdue
  The senseless marble to such forms of truth,
And mould the semblance of Earth's chosen few
  To an enduring shape and second youth;
Bequeath his features, whose emphatic page
Will nerve the spirits of a future age!

XI.

SPRING.

Why fall the bonds of custom from us now,
  And wonted scenes with virgin glory teem?
While tender memories o'ershade the brow,
  And life grows sweet and solemn as a dream?
Spring to the earth has come; her fountains leap,
  In fields of azure pearly clouds repose,
Meek flowers seem along the turf to creep,
  And long the lingering twilight softly glows;
The unfettered streams to ocean's bosom rush,
  Warm are the sands the radiant billows lave,
The foam-crests glisten with a brighter flush,
  And childhood's sportive mood sways wind and
      wave;
Music and balm upon the air float free,
As if with youth renewed came immortality!

XII.

TO PIUS IX.

IN 1848.

Benign Reformer! thy sublime career
  Has taught the rulers a forgotten art, —
That Truth may palsy Valor's arm with fear,
  And nerve a priest to act a hero's part;
Achieve thy purpose, give a nation birth,
  Vain is the Jesuit wile, the Austrian steel;
That sceptre which so long betrayed the earth,
  In thy pure hands is swayed for human weal;
The world with benedictions breathes thy name,
  And hails the Vatican as Freedom's home,
With bloodless triumphs thou hast won a fame
  More wide and stainless than the sky of Rome,
Thy effigies a glorious challenge fling
From Beauty's robe and Wisdom's signet ring.

XIII.

TO THE SAME.

IN 1849.

O, HAD it been thy lot that hour to die,
  The Pantheon would boast a dearer name
Than all who there oblivion defy!
  Now thou hast won the cruel bigot's fame;
Apostate, crouching in a tyrant's lair
  From the just hate of those thou hast betrayed,
The craven fears of regal allies share,
  And shun the hecatomb thy baseness made!
Thou art the skeleton at Freedom's feast,
  To which thy voice so blandly called the world.
How soon the man was vanquished by the priest,
  And in the dust the faith of nations hurled!
God speeds the new crusade for human rights,
While patient scorn thy cowardice requites.

XIV.

ON THE DEATH OF ALLSTON.

THE element of beauty which in thee
  Was a prevailing spirit, pure and high,
And from all guile had made thy being free,
  Now seems to whisper thou canst never die!
For Nature's priests we shed no idle tear,
  Their mantles on a noble lineage fall;
Though thy white locks at length have pressed the bier,
  Death could not fold thee in Oblivion's pall:
Majestic forms thy hand in grace arrayed,
  Eternal watch shall keep beside thy tomb,
And hues aerial that thy pencil stayed,
  Its shades with Heaven's radiance illume;
Art's meek apostle, holy is thy sway,
From the heart's records ne'er to pass away!

XV.

FROM THE ITALIAN.

In a fair garden grew a purple rose,
  Shedding abroad an odor fresh and rare ;
A nymph beholding, with sweet transport glows,
  And at the winsome sight exclaims "How fair!"
Her gentle hand to pluck it she extends,
  But envious thorns are hid beneath its leaves:
As o'er it with a trustful joy she bends,
  A sudden wound her ardent grasp deceives.
"Alas!" she murmurs, "now the truth I feel,
  That beauty ever is allied to pain,
Life's richest music discords will reveal,
  And every blessing hath its kindred bane."
"Yes," I replied, "thyself doth prove it true;
For thou art lovely and yet cruel too."

XVI.

THE BASSO-RELIEVO OF JUPITER AND HEBE.

Poised on his mighty wings, Jove's kingly bird
Stoops to the cup luxurious Hebe fills;
All day those wings the empyrean have stirred,
But now each plume a soft enchantment thrills:
The lone and weary monarch of the skies
Lapt in content, imbibes the draught of Love,
By gentle hands, and tender, watchful eyes,
Nurtured to soar Ambition's flight above.
Fondly majestic bending o'er the urn
Exhaustless as her sympathetic breast,
With calm delight see the fair goddess turn,
Dispensing feel the rapture of her guest,
To show how poor unshared is Nature's wealth
While Love to noble souls alone is health.

XVII.

TO JENNY LIND.

A MELODY with Southern passion fraught
  I hear thee warble : 'tis as if a bird
By intuition human strains had caught,
  But whose pure breast no kindred feeling stirred.
Thy native song the hushed arena fills,
  So wildly plaintive, that I seem to stand
Alone, and see, from off the circling hills,
  The bright horizon of the North expand!
High art is thus intact; and matchless skill
  Born of intelligence and self-control, —
The graduated tone and perfect trill
  Prove a restrained, but not a frigid soul;
Thine finds expression in such generous deeds,
That music from thy lips for human sorrow pleads!

XVIII.

DESOLATION.

THINK ye the desolate must live apart,
By solemn vows to convent-walls confined?
Ah! no; with men may dwell the cloister'd heart,
And in a crowd the isolated mind;
Tearless behind the prison-bars of fate,
The world sees not how desolate they stand,
Gazing so fondly through the iron grate
Upon the promised yet forbidden land;
Patience, the shrine to which their bleeding feet
Day after day in voiceless penance turn;
Silence, the holy cell and calm retreat,
In which unseen their meek devotions burn;
Life is to them a vigil which none share,
Their hopes a sacrifice, their love a prayer.

XIX.

STEINHAUSEN'S HERO AND LEANDER.

FAINT from the wave, each nerve by toil unstrung,
  Behold life mantle in his glowing face
With the delight that cannot find a tongue,
  How vain are words to yield expression place,
When the instinctive grasp, the yielding form,
  The lips that seem to quiver with content,
So well proclaim the haven in life's storm —
  The heart's goal reached—the kindred spirits blent!
Let the cold spray lave their unconscious feet,
  And time bring round the parting hour again,
Now Love's pure triumph is once more complete,
  And present joy oblivious of pain;
As in enraptured silence, heart meets heart,
Genius the moment seized to consecrate for Art!

XX.

DELAROCHE'S PICTURE

OF NAPOLEON CROSSING THE ALPS.

Unconscious of the dreary wastes around,
Of sleet that pierces with each fitful blast,
The icy peaks, the rough and treacherous ground,
Huge snow-drifts by the whirlwind's breath amassed,
Through which the jaded mule with noiseless tread,
Patient and slow, a certain foothold seeks,
By the old peasant-guide so meekly led;
Moves the wan conqueror, with sunken cheeks,
O'er heights as cold and lonely as his soul,—
The chill lips blandly set, and the dark eyes
Intent with fierce ambition's vast control,
Sad, keen, and thoughtful of the distant prize;
With the imperial robes and warlike steed,
That face ne'er wore such blended might and need!

XXI.

ALLEGHANIA.

Worthy the patriot's thought and poet's lyre,
  This second baptism of our native earth,
To consecrate anew her manhood's fire,
  By a true watchword all of mountain-birth;
For to the hills has Freedom ever clung,
  And their proud name should designate the free;
That when its echoes through the land are rung,
  Her children's breasts may warm to liberty!
My country! in the van of nations thou
  Art called to raise Truth's lonely banner high;
'Tis fit a noble title grace thy brow,
  Born of thy race, beneath thy matchless sky
And Alps and Appenines resign their fame,
When thrills the world's deep heart with Alleghania's
    name!

XXII.

O FOR a castle on a woodland height!
  High mountains round, and a pure stream below,
Within all charms that tasteful hours invite,
  Wise books of poesy and music's flow;—
A grassy lawn through which to course our steeds,
  A gothic chapel in seclusion reared,
Where we could solace find for holiest needs,
  And grow by mutual rites the more endeared:
How such captivity alone with thee
  Would lift to Paradise each passing day!
Then all revealed my patient love would be,
  And thou couldst not a full response delay:
For Truth makes holy Love's illusive dreams,
And their best promise constantly redeems.

XXIII.

THE rain-drops patter on the casement still,
  So hushed the room each faint watch-tick I hear,
The crackling of the embers seems to fill
  This brooding quiet with an accent clear:
I've looked awhile upon the gifted page,
  Glanced at the dingy roofs and leaden sky,
Or paced the floor my mind to disengage,
  Chiding the languid hours as they fly;
In vain! the thought of thee o'ermasters all,
  Now waking joy, and now a dark surmise,
As memory spreads her banquet or her pall,
  And bids me hopeless sink or gladsome rise:
On what bright wings these lonely hours would flee,
Dared I but feel that thou hast thought of me!

XXIV.

What though our dream is broken? Yet again
 Like a familiar angel it shall bear
Consoling treasures for these days of pain,
 Such as they only who have grieved can share;
As unhived nectar for the bee to sip,
 Lurks in each flower-cell which the spring-time
  brings,
As music rests upon the quiet lip,
 And power to soar yet lives in folded wings,
So let the love on which our spirits glide,
 Flow deep and strong beneath its bridge of sighs,
No shadow resting on the latent tide
 Whose heaven-ward current baffles human eyes,
Until we stand upon the holy shore,
And realms it prophesied, at length explore.

XXV.

In my first youth, the feverish thirst for gain
   That in this noble land makes life so chill,
Was tempered to a wiser trust by pain,
   Hope's early blight, — a chastening sense of ill;
And I was exiled to a sunny clime,
   Where cloud and flower a softer meaning caught
From graceful forms and holy wrecks of time,
   Appealing all to fond and pensive thought;
Enamored of the Beautiful I grew,
   And at her altar pledged my virgin soul, —
O let me here those treasured vows renew,
   And thou the service shalt henceforth control;
For in thy graces and thy love sincere
Lives the blest spirit that I yet revere.

XXVI.

Courage and patience! elements whereby
  My soul shall yet her citadel maintain,
Baffled, perplexed, and struggling oft to fly
  Far, far above this realm of wasting pain,—
Come with your still and banded vigor now,
  Fill my sad breast with energy divine,
Stamp a firm thought upon my aching brow,
  Make my impulsive visions wholly thine,
Freeze my pent tears, chill all my tender dreams,
  Brace my weak heart in panoply sublime;
Till dwelling only on my martyr themes,
  And, turning from the richest lures of time,
Love, like an iceberg of the polar deep,
In adamantine rest is laid asleep.

XXVII.

> "My mind's the same
> It ever was to you. Where I find worth
> I love the keeper, till he let it go,
> And then I follow it." — *Old Play.*

Like the fair sea that laves Italia's strand,
  Affection's flood is tideless in my breast;
No ebb withdraws it from the chosen land,
  Havened too richly for enamored quest:
Thus am I faithful to the vanished grace
  Embodied once in thy sweet form and name,
And though love's charm no more illumes thy face,
  In memory's realm her olden pledge I claim.
It is not constancy to haunt a shrine
  From which devotion's lingering spark has fled;
Insensate homage only wreaths can twine
  Around the pulseless temples of the dead:
Thou from thy better self hast madly flown,
While to that self allegiance still I own.

XXVIII.

The buds have opened, and in leafy pride
Woo the soft winds of this capricious May;
With a refreshing green the fields are dyed,
And clearer sparkles on the waters play.
All Nature speaks of boundless promise now,
In tones as sweet as thine,—her hand is laid
With a maternal greeting on my brow,
Until its fevered throbbings all are stayed;
And I am fain to lie upon her breast,
Unconscious of the world, divorced from pain,
Drink from her rosy lips the balm of rest,
And be her glad and trustful child again:
But such fond dalliance claims a spirit free,
And all her spells are broken—without thee!

XXIX.

SEMPRE LO STESSO.

Ever the same ! — let this our watchword be
  Upon the dreary battlements of time,
With a clear soul I breathe it unto thee
  In tones whose fervor mocks this idle rhyme ;
Ever the same ; — how sweet to earn with pain
  The tested love that casteth out all fear,
And amid all we suffer, doubt and feign,
  To own one true and self-absorbing sphere !
Ever the same ; — as moons the waters draw,
  A simple presence calms all inward strife,
And, by the sway of some benignant law,
  With high completeness fills the sense of life :
The Holy One this sacred thought confest
When leaning on his fond disciple's breast.

www.ingramcontent.com/pod-product-compliance
Lightning Source LLC
LaVergne TN
LVHW011223110826
845150LV00006B/1519

* 9 7 8 1 4 2 5 5 1 5 6 7 6 *